PHONE PIRATE

A Cautionary Tale

By

Vadim Viktorov

First publication 2018

R23 Publishing

R23MRJ@gmail.com

DISCLAIMER

This book is a work of fiction. Although its form is that of an autobiography, it is not one. Space and Time have been rearranged to suit the convenience of the book, and with the exception of public figures, any resemblance to persons living or dead is coincidental. The opinions expressed are those of the character's and should not be confused within the author's

Contents

Some Stuff You Need To Know 2

Calle Aribau 7

Rambla Catalunya 53

Ronda San Pere 97

Calle de la Diputacio 141

Lower East Side Sushi & Drinks 208

Afterword – A Message from the Author 241

"You cannot expect loyalty from people who will do anything for money"

Some Stuff You Need To Know

So here's the gig, pay attention and all will become as clear as mud.

So, small privately held U.S corporate entities, companies in other words, issue shares of stock, including freely traded shares that are what are considered or referred to as over-the-counter trades. These trades are reported on the over-the-counter bulletin board, or pink sheets. The OTCBB and pink sheets are quotation medians that contain quotations for thousands of OTC stocks not listed on any of the major stock markets. Still with me? Kind of boring right? Well hang around.

These same small, privately held corporate entities can also issue what are referred to as restricted shares which as the name suggests cannot be freely traded. This stock is also referred to as Regulation S. These Reg S shares are restricted to purchasers outside the U.S that are non-U.S citizens. The restriction on these shares also includes a period of time where the shares cannot be sold. A hold period in other words which is usually between 12-24 months.

Sales of Reg S shares are not reported on the OTCBB or pink sheets and consequently because of this restriction and the cost and work involved in lifting the restriction, together with the fact that many of these small privately held corporate entities have very low volumes of turnover of their freely traded shares makes the value of Reg S shares difficult to determine. Certainly however, they are considered to be far less valuable than their freely trading cousins. Some would go as far as to say that they're not worth the paper they're printed on.

My name is John Robson and together with my business partner Al Parker, I ran a high-pressure tele-sales operation, sometimes referred to as a Boiler Room, from various location in Barcelona, Spain. From this operation our callers contacted prospective investors in order to sell restricted Reg S shares using high-pressure tactics, fraudulent statements, misleading representations and false promises in order to make the value of the potential investment appear far greater than was actually the reality of the situation.

Hell, we made the potential for substantial profit sound fucking outstanding when in fact the vast majority of these companies were crying out for infusions of capital, or to put it slightly more bluntly, were on the bones of their collective asses. In fact they had as much chance of reaching the potential we so convincingly professed as I did of sprouting a pair of angel's wings.

These activities took place between spring 2006 until the summer of 2010. We operated under many different guises including Oxbridge International, Glamorgan Global,

International Energy Partners and Hampton Equity Group. Shares were obtained through our Florida based stock provider, a 50 something ex-stock broker by the name of Herb Silver at twenty five cents on the dollar.

During the period of our operation we obtained and sold shares to an unsuspecting public, restricted shares of course, issued by various companies including International Holding Corporation, United Energy Corporation, Lion Outdoor International, and Clean Fuel Technologies Inc.

Most of the time these shares were sold to investors without disclosing the fact they were restricted and leading investors to believe they were in fact purchasing freely trading shares. Our terms and conditions stated of course that the shares were restricted but hey, who reads terms and conditions when they've bought a story hook line and sinker?

Along with Herb Silver a guy by the name of Greg Kole, an accountant, and Joe Milan, a securities lawyer helped facilitate what can only be described as a large international scam, a rip off, or to put it as one T.V investigative documentary termed it, The Great British Share Swindle.

Here's my story of those years.

Calle Aribau

I arrived in Barcelona in February 2005. After reading the introduction to this book the last thing you'll want to do is take advice from me. Nevertheless I'll give it anyway. If you've never been to Barcelona, then go. It's truly a fantastic city. From its Gothic and Gaudi inspired architecture, its exquisite and varied cuisine, its bohemian yet chic attitude, to its glorious coastal location and almost perfect climate, Barcelona captured my heart immediately. It excites all the senses, it's a city that's alive, pulsating yet moving to its own unique beat and unlike London, New York or Paris, retains much of a small town Catalan personality. It is passionately Catalan as opposed to the Spanishness of Valencia, Madrid or Seville and a city I'll always love. It's also a city from where plenty of my dreams were realised and from where I shattered the dreams of many.

I'd been in the 'business' since early 2000 where, after answering an ad in a national tabloid I flew out to join a firm in Kuala Lumpur, Malaysia. After a few short months that firm ran into some legal challenges and upped sticks moving the whole deal out to Cyprus where I dutifully followed.

Differences of opinion saw me leave that gig and drift around Asia before making my move to Spain. I was chilling out on one of the many beautiful Philippine Islands drinking plenty of cold beer in long days filled with lots of sun, sea and sex when I received a call from an South African by the name of Nad Fala. I'd never met Nad nor knew of him, though he knew of me through friends of friends which was often the case as to how positions were offered and secured within the dirty business. The staffing of Boiler Rooms has always been an under the radar kind of activity.

The conversation between Nad and I was easy, flowing and natural. Nad was making all the right noises and sounded organised, professional and ambitious. Nad and his two associates, the bosses, were setting up an operation in Barcelona and wanted me closing for them. This was a brand new opportunity, and in fact they wouldn't be ready for me for a few weeks. Over the course of the next two weeks I spoke from my tropical paradise via that magnificent invention, the telephone, to Nad's two bosses; Italian American Tony Rossi (Big Tony) and John Trout, a Brazilian with not much of a Brazilian sounding name (JT).

The group had been operating a successful currency trading (FX) business in Barcelona for a couple of years. By successful I mean successful for Big Tony and JT. It corruptly generated tens of millions of dollars for the pair and complete losses for all its clients. Yep, complete and all.

The pair had their hearts set on setting up a Reg S stock sales business and they wanted yours truly closing business as prolifically as my reputation suggested I could. My reputation as a top closer went before me and JT and the Big Man made it clear that they wanted me. They made me an offer I couldn't refuse, or at least I didn't want to.

Perfect timing was in play. I was restless for a new opportunity and after my recent telephone conversations with these guys I was itching to get back in the saddle. Within three days of my last telephone conversation with Big Tony I found myself sipping champagne in Business Class winging my way to the Catalan capital courtesy of my new bosses. I was pretty damn excited to see Barcelona and the quality apartment that was being provided for me rent free as part of the deal.

It quickly became apparent that Big Tony and JT were major players in the Boiler Room game within the city, albeit in

FX as opposed to Reg S, though that was all about to change. The two were absolutely raking it in. Tony looked more like a heavyweight boxer than the smart business man that he was, while JT had Hollywood good looks and loved to party like a rock star. From the moment I arrived, I felt like I had 'arrived'. I was 'in' with a serious crew who certainly seemed to have it going on.

Senor Alonso, one of the firms fixers, met me at El Prat International Airport in a gleaming black Mercedes and chauffeured me to my temporary but perfectly adequate accommodation on Calle Balmes as it crossed Calle Aragon right in the centre of the city. At the apartment Senor Alonso handed me over, so to speak, to Paulo Vilchez Caluso, the firm's Costa Rican security guy. Paulo showed me into my fifth floor apartment explaining that most of the apartments in the building were rented by the firm to house staff from the currency office and newly recruited staff for the just opened share sales office. As a closer I'd been allocated a one bedroom apartment to myself whereas fronters (cold callers) were sharing in two and three bedroom units. Paulo lived in one of the apartments as well, tasked by Tony to show new people in, as he was doing with me, and to throw useless people out as well as putting out all sorts of fires and keeping a bunch of drunken and drug crazed phone pirates in line. Paulo did a good job it seemed and possessed various restraining equipment (and weaponry) in order to assist him in his role.

Within my first month at the new office on Calle Aribau it became clear that my ability as a top closer was real and not mere folk lore. JT showed his appreciation by letting me know that one of the girls was actively looking for a more suitable apartment for someone of my ability. No complaints from me, we all like smoke blown up our arses at one time or another.

The office on Aribau to the casual observer looked perhaps like an architect's office or maybe some tech start-up. High ceilings with ornate coving, stripped heavy timber doors, rich polished floorboards all contrasted with lots of mirrors, leather and chrome. It was a really cool office, not only in its professional executive feel but in the efficient way it ran.

I'd been used to working in various utilitarian type offices and been used to prospecting for my own clients by trawling through endless lead lists making hundreds of calls daily in search of prospects I could sell to. Here however, I was one of two closers, each of us with a team of four fronters, all churning out qualified leads like machines. Very quickly I came to realise that without a shadow of doubt this was the best gig I had ever worked at. No cold calling, simply closing. I started making great money from the get-go.

Al, the other closer, and my future partner in crime arrived at the office the day after I did and we very quickly hit it off. My first impression of Al was that of a boss. He had a commanding air about him, mid-fifties, tall, tanned, cropped hair and gestapo blue eyes. Dressed smartly but casually that including a camel hair coat he reminded me of a mob guy, especially with his gruff New York drawl and quick wit. I think he probably thought the same about me, or the equivalent on the other side of the pond although I must confess I've never had the inclination to throw on a camel hair coat. Regardless, and like I said, we hit it off straight away.

Working together at the Aribau office was always a blast with Al. Left to our own devices there was plenty of on-the-job humour whilst both proving to be incredibly productive. Outside of the office we spend a large chunk of time together as well, which revolved around drinking, some recreational drugs and chasing beautiful women around this fantastic city. I recall one of Al's fronters, a teetotaller named Sean piping up after one of Al's riotously funny tales that generally speaking revolved around social settings involving alcohol, suggesting that they hang out together sometime. Without missing a beat Al fired back "and do what?". For sure, our way of life outside the office was lived at high speed and high velocity. It became a passion, an obsession, and a way of life, not merely a wind-down at the end of the day. We were full on. Neither of us either ever cried off sick after a night of excess, both staying true to the unwritten rule 'boys go out at night but men come to work in the morning'. And work we did, hitting the phones hard, day in day out writing deal after deal after deal.

Standard practice was to open accounts for between $5000-$10,000, of what we considered small, or schoolboy trades. Once clients funds had cleared our job then was to set-up the client for enhancement, or what is termed 'the load'. This was the most important part of the process. A successful set-up would achieve a number of things, such as the credibility of the loader, who'd be referred to in the set-up process as Head of Global Equities or President of Emerging Equities or something as equally grand. Complete crap of course. The goal being to create such an aura of mythical greatness around the loader's ability that when I would drop into the conversation that this god of a man was actually willing to do me a favour and speak to my client, the client would feel like Warren Buffet himself was about to give him some breaking news and would drop or at the very least rearrange any other pressing engagements he had lined up. We would also create scenarios that would suggest that the client's involvement in the opportunity couldn't have been timed better and that big things, really big things, were happening. "I'm not sure what the breaking news is Mike but I can tell you that there has never been such a buzz about the office. All sorts of top guys are showing up from the States and the word is that there's a huge amount of money to be made on this one" Obviously the idea behind all the hype was to excite the client to such a degree that he'd sell his wife and kids if necessary to fund an additional and more substantial opportunity should he be privileged enough to be invited to partake.

Our loader, probably one of the best in the business, was a New Jersey Jew, Jack Portman. Ruthless, obnoxious and incredibly effective. Al once set-up an Australian client who'd informed Al that he was going to borrow the money for the load from a very dangerous source and that if he didn't repay them in full with interest within six months he'd be up shit creek without a paddle. Or probably more to the point, up shit creek without a paddle and wearing a pair of concrete boots. When Al relayed this information to Jack, Jack's response was an immediate and serious "hey, don't go soft on me now Al". I believe the guy did load and perhaps dropped off the radar several months later. We were involved in a ruthless game and would hit clients over and over with the object being to bleed them completely dry. As Al liked to say "I tell all my clients that if they stick with me I'll make them a small fortune" quickly followed up with " they may start out with a big fortune but hey.." In the year or so I spent with this outfit the best (not for the client) load I was involved with was from an account I'd opened for $12,000. He went on to load for a cool $1,000,000. Commission payouts have gone up since 2005 and at that stage I made 5% on the load, so $50,000. My fronter who had created the confirmed lead in the first place got five points too, while Jack got ten. So on this deal the bosses paid out $200,000 in commission to three individuals. Pretty generous I'm sure you'll agree. But put into the context that Big Tony and JT were buying the stock for no more than $250,000 meant that after paying those generous commissions they were splitting $550,000 between the pair of them. Nice work if you can get it. They of course had the expense of running the office and its associated costs, but still.

Al had his fair share of sizeable loads too, and I felt sure the wheels were turning in his head as much as they were in mine, wondering about the feasibility of going it alone. But I'm jumping ahead of myself.

Within six weeks of arriving in Spain I was offered and accepted a beautiful rent-free apartment on Rambla Catalunya, one of the most stunning streets in the city, and that's not just my opinion, Ernest Hemingway thought so too.

I very quickly pimped out my new gaff with the latest T.V's, sound system, quality furniture and artwork. The end result much to my liking – a spectacular bachelor pad. I'd settled into life in this wonderful city and was enjoying every damn minute of it.

Although the work was virtually all phone based there were a handful of occasions when Al and I went to meet clients. The meetings were to strengthen our chances of closing larger deals when a client happened to be in the city. Although any occasion where a fancy restaurant and copious amounts of fine wine are flowing tends to blur the line between business and pleasure. The three meeting I remember in particular were all held in great restaurants, were great fun and resulted in the three clients collectively investing just shy of two million dollars.

One client brought his extremely attractive Romanian girlfriend to our dinner meeting. On the way to the restaurant in the taxi with already a few drinks on board Al informed me that he'd told his client I was a hedge fund manager. "What do hedge fund managers do?" I asked. "Manage hedge funds Champ, manage hedge funds" came Al's truthful reply. That said, and as I've never been shy of shooting from the hip, we bowled into the restaurant.

As the evening drew on Al was getting deeper into conversation with his client whom he was sat opposite while I was getting deeper into conversation with the client's very hot Romanian 'friend' who all of a sudden slipped off her shoe and started rubbing my leg with her foot. If there had not been so much money at stake I might have swiped her away from him for myself. In hindsight the client perhaps would have preferred that rather than losing the $600,000 that he did. I felt pretty sure the Romanian was a paid 'girlfriend' but for certain, the client took the biggest shafting that night without a doubt.

Life moved along nicely that first year with several events conspiring to draw Al and I closer to branching out on our own. That autumn, news came to the office that Big Tony had been arrested and charged in Florida. J.T supported by Nad held extensive meeting with us all to bring us up to speed with unfolding events and put to bed any fears anyone may have that we were going to get busted too. Basically, Tony had formed a foreign currency trading operation in the late nineties that was so rigged, and with the man working behind the curtain against the clients best interests, that all clients basically had the asses handed to them. Tony and his associates had been charged in a multi-million dollar fraud that ultimately saw Tony doing a nine stretch. Prior to sentencing however he was out on bail but unable to travel. J.T assured everyone that there was no connection between Tony's business in the States and our business in Barcelona. These assurances spewed from J.T's mouth like a projectile vomiter. Like that crazy chick in the Exorcist.

As anticipated Tony dropped off the radar shortly after and J.T was the new king. The king is dead, long live the king. And not long after that the currency office in Barcelona closed down with some of the staff going elsewhere but a fair chunk of them coming over to learn how to sell Reg S stock. The influx of new faces meant we'd outgrown the really cool office on Aribau and were moved to bigger offices up the street.

Here Al and I were two of four closers, though our seniority was implied by us being given our own separate office with sliding double doors that we could keep open to watch the room and encourage our teams of fronters, or close for a quieter atmosphere in which to ply our trade. Or in fact, to conspire.

The new office although only a couple of blocks up Aribau from the old, never really captured the atmosphere and excitement of the original Aribau room. The influx of currency guys into the Reg S office created a somewhat of an us and them feel to some degree and of course, Big Tony's absence was felt by all. J.T and Nad held pretty good sales meeting at the start of every day but Big Tony's off the cuff power meetings couldn't be rivalled. The décor and furniture in the new office were perfectly adequate but the polished finesse of the original Aribau office, like Tony, was clearly absent.

I was tasked with holding training sessions with the new currency guys over the first few weeks of their coming together with us Reg S boys, they did start performing and after a while began to fit in. Everyone was making money but something was missing. I'm not complaining though, I was still having a ball and making more money than any of the other closers, Al included. I even made $20,000 in my absence while spending ten days in the Philippines as a few of my clients loaded while I was away. That trip was fun with a capital F. I met a singer in Hard Rock Café in Makati City and whisked her away to Boracay a beautiful island retreat for a couple of days. Jaz was great fun and sexy as hell with lips to equal Angelina Jolie's and gravity defying tits. I'm not sure if they are still quite as perky these days as she's now married to an Italian with a couple of little Italians in tow while living in Italy funnily enough. Anyway, that trip is another story, suffice to say when the text hit my phone informing me that I'd just made another $20,000 I was as happy as a pig in shit. I was in a casino on a bit of a roll with the delicious Jaz and just couldn't seem to lose. A good night was had by all. Memorable I think they call it.

Christmas came and went and my high-velocity life of work, drink, drugs and girls continued in its endlessly enjoyable loop. Then in early spring J.T invited me to lunch. He had a proposition.

I took a taxi from the office to Arts Hotel, one of the most exclusive in Barcelona, located in Port Olympic and a regular haunt for the visiting rich and famous. I met J.T at the bar and we quickly moved to one of the hotels fabulous restaurants. J.T was fast talking and full of it, he'd lived in Miami for most of his life though had been born and spent his first few years in San Paulo, Brazil. He neither looked or sounded Brazilian and was never one to beat around the bush. His proposal was delivered in a simple and straightforward manner. J.T had an office lease he had secured through Albert Marvin that was now surplus to requirements. Albert (Fat Albi) Marvin of Albert Marvin & Associates was based out of the original Aribau office and ran an ex-pat services company that arranged everything from local and off-shore company formations, bank introductions, property sourcing, lease negotiation, residency applications, accountancy and payroll services amongst other stuff. Basically anything an ex-pat might require. Albi did not work directly for Tony or J.T but might as well have considering the amount of work they put his way.

The office J.T was talking about was located on Rambla Catalunya a stone's throw from my apartment. J.T had set the office up a few months previously as a prescription meds tele-sales business that never took off. FastMeds had not succeeded and the office was now empty of people, but tele-sales ready. J.T was offering me banking, stock and no up-front costs to walk into this office and set up shop. I would just pick up the ongoing expenses once I was in. He'd sign over the company FastMeds SL so I could operate legally in Spain and I'd be free to create my own website using whatever names I deemed fit. I'd pay all commission to my staff and salary to an admin girl but could put all trades through J.T's admin staff at the Aribau office and I'd be paid 40% of all money my office raised. It would be a lot more responsibility but a challenge I felt up for nonetheless.

Al had recently started loading at the Aribau office as Jack Portman had recently done one, taking half the old currency boys with him to set up shop elsewhere in the city and going back into the currency game. J.T's offer also included having Al loading for my office if I so wished.

My immediate challenge was how to staff the place as obviously J.T didn't plan on me taking guys from the Aribau office. I didn't have the financial wherewithal or inclination to embark on a underground advertising campaign, to fly guys in, pay them a weekly advance on commission until they became productive (if at all) and to house the animals in apartments throughout the city. I'd be biting off more than I could chew. That said, I had an idea.

Jeff Rogers had arrived in Barcelona a year before me. We had worked together in Malaysia and Indonesia in the past and even taken a trip to Australia together. We'd become good friends and had gotten up to some wild things in Asia. Jeff was working for a different crew and had actually tried to get me to jump ship within days of my arrival in Barcelona. We'd met at Café 7 just across from my apartment at the time and a few beers turned into an all-nighter. Although we kept in touch, perhaps meeting for dinner and drinks, maybe even snagging a couple of hookers and a bag of blow, the business was very tribal and different crews didn't tend to socialise together.

I knew Jeff was doing OK and I knew he had a following of eight or nine guys that would potentially come with him if I could get him to leave his current gig to come with me.

Obviously I'd need to make the prospect attractive enough. So I thought it through and set up a meeting.

We met at the usual haunt, Café 7, like I said, I'd put a lot of thought into this and was looking forward to pitching Jeff on the idea of partnering up in a gig of our own and working together once again.

Bingo. After an hour of pitching the idea and a bit of a Q & A session Jeff was sold and committed to come on board feeling confident he could bring at least six guys with him, and knew others around the city he could hit up as well. Seeing as the meeting had gone so well we didn't feel like ending it at that point, especially as café 7 hadn't run out of beer, and Gauchos, that fabulous Argentinian steak house located just across Calle Aragon less than a minute's walk from our current location beckoned.

The very next morning J.T and Nad dropped a bombshell. The offshore bank account that our clients sent their funds to had been frozen. In their morning meeting J.T and Nad played it down as much as they could assuring us that the freeze was not due to any illegal activity and started bigging up the potential of the shares we were promoting and the very likely massive returns our clients would see. According to J.T the freeze was unnecessary and unrelated to our business and had something to do with something or other within the bank bla bla bla on he went. The long and the short of this disastrous situation was that the closers needed to get on the phone immediately and convince any clients about to send money to hang on for another 72 hours or so as we would now be issuing new bank instructions. We span this as a benefit to the client inasmuch as we'd tell them that the $150 administration fee we charged clients due to banking costs we were exposed to as a company were being eliminated as we were getting a much better deal through a new clearing agent that would allow us to eliminate the $150 fee completely. Basically another offshore account set up by Albert Marvin. We'd continue the spin by saying this new clearing agent had been courting us for our business for quite some time and had now effectively won it by offering a superior service and then reminding them again that we would now be doing away with the administration fee we had traditionally passed onto clients and this was all part of our so-called ongoing policy of reducing costs and improving profits. All of this was obviously a crock of shit and was designed to steer the clients attention away from the simple fact that our banking had actually been frozen, pending an investigation into our business activities. Those calls were the easy calls we needed to make. The more difficult calls that needed an extra dollop of bullshit were the calls in which we needed to ask the client to contact their banks and request their bank recall their funds that had already been sent to our so-called clearing agent and when they received the funds back to resend them again to our new so-called clearing agent. Fuck a duck, it was hard enough going through the whole process of building confidence and trust with a client in order to get him or her to send money in the first place let alone having to call them up and tell them to recall the money they were probably nervous about sending in the first place and then get them to go through the whole nerve jangling experience again of sending their funds into the unknown, the black hole, the abyss. It was hard to believe that J.T didn't have alternative banking already waiting in the wings. What a mug.

Nevertheless, shooting from the hip and putting a super spin on things had always been a forte, so off I dialled. Calls would go something like this. "Hi Dave, it's John (me), listen

Dave I have to apologise and I'm going to need you to do something for me. My secretary, dozy cow, sent you in error the wrong wiring instructions, in fact she sent you the wiring instructions we use for our institutional clients and we would be breaking all sorts of regulations if we cleared your funds through that route. I know it's an absolute pain in the arse Dave but I'm going to need you to recall those funds, if we wait on it getting sorted out in the system it's going to take weeks and I don't want you to miss out on any profits we may see in the very short term and I can only hold the price we agreed for the stock for a few more days, tops. Listen Dave, we'll obviously compensate you for any charges you incur and I'm also going to waive the $150 administration fee too and get you compensated for that, fair enough?" And without waiting for his response "please get on this right away, OK Dave?" Confidence and a matter of fact attitude whilst being instructive can work wonders and meant that I lost zero deals during this complete balls up.

But wait, there's more. More bad news that is. Or at least what could be construed as bad news unless the super-spin went into full effect. How does the saying go, perception is everything, right? Later that day Nad was tasked with the unpleasant job of dropping a second bombshell, shit it was like the frigging damn busters that day. I guess J.T was all bombed out and happy to leave the task to Nad while he hid away in the air raid shelter of Albert Marvin's office working on a new bank account, or probably more accurately, nagging Albert Martin to get it done sooner than was humanly possible.

This next bombshell was that with immediate effect the stock we'd been selling was no longer available. And, yes you guessed it, to include all the clients who were recalling money and waiting to be given new instructions on where to send it once it was safely back in their bank accounts. We'd sold these clients on the idea of a promising looking biotech company and now we needed to tell them they couldn't have it. Great. But hey, we had something a million times better for them. A shitty online dating company. Brilliant.

Al and I decided immediately and in unison that this latest news would go no further until the clients had resent their funds to the new bank once it appeared. At that stage we'd flip them into this garbage looking online dating company that was no Tinder for sure. Through all this messing about however, this unexpected hiccup presented an opportunity that would change everything and act as a catalyst to the development of mine and Al's business relationship.

Back at the old office when Tony had been around he had once called Al and I into see him to present us with what he referred to as a gift. Tony had a very easy way about him and I had only ever seen him wearing sweat pants t-shirt and sneakers, even when those around him were suited and booted. Anyway, Tony's gift was basically a client who had invested $4 million through his currency room and lost it all. No surprise there. Most of that injection of cash to Tony's bank account had gone into building his mansion in Boca Raton, Florida. Apparently it had the biggest indoor saltwater aquarium in the State built into one of the walls that was home to a number of four foot long sharks. Not surprisingly the client who had contributed so much to Tony's mansion was done with currencies but Tony felt he was still up for it in a different game. The Reg S game. As it happens, he wasn't wrong. Working as a tag team Al and I extracted another $500,000 from our gift over the course of the next several months.

Now, at the time of J.T and Nad's announcement, you remember, the couple or three bombshells they landed on us concerning a frozen bank account and the end of our nice little biotech stock to promote and the introduction of the worst online dating site in the history of the world for us to sell instead. Well, at the time Al and I had been preparing our gift for a $200,000 deal. He was hot to trot and waiting for my promised call to bring him the good news either that very morning or tomorrow morning at the very latest. I had no intention of sitting on it another 24 hours and had left my call back a little ambiguous purposely but knowing full well I was going in today. Now we were expected to sit on our hands waiting for this new bank account to materialise. The fact that the stock was changing from the biotech company to the worst online dating company in the world was not an issue where the gift was concerned as I had also purposely held back specifics of the opportunity he was about to shovel two hundred big ones into in order to create that sense of urgency and belief that this was a brand new hot issue and exclusive to those in the most knowing of knows. But here was I all jacked up with no one to phone, ready to give him the green light and pin his hat on but with nowhere for him to send his cash. I had no choice but to call him and tell him the meetings were still in progress and to hang on. For the remainder of that day we made all the life saver calls and got the results we set out to do. Recalls, holds, flips and promises of resends once funds were safely back in the client's accounts. By 5pm I was ready for the off so when Al looked over and said he had an idea, I was already half wayout of the door. Little did I know that when Al said he had an idea that he was suggesting anything other than a few cold ones at Café 7 and maybe smoke a bone or two. But that was soon to change.

We took our usual spot outside to watch the world, and more precisely Barcelona's beautiful females float by. A perfect pastime while supping a cold one and sharing a joint. We discussed the days events and both felt that J.T and Nad had really dropped the ball on this one and let us all down unnecessarily. It wasn't their first rodeo for fuck sake. They'd been in the business long enough to know this sort of thing could happen and should have had alternative banking ready. No excuses. To top off this monumental fuck up we had also had to back pedal on the stock we'd been pushing as we'd lost it for whatever reason with no warning at all. And the new stock, the dating company, Jesus. There were also rumours circulating that J.T was stiffing Tony. They had been equal partners in the Barcelona set-up and the word was that J.T had completely cut Tony off now that he was stuck in Florida and facing some serious fed time.

The beers were going down nicely on this very pleasant spring evening when Al suggested an alternative scenario concerning our gift. He explained two things. First, if we decided to go this route we'd make a hell of a lot more than the $20,000 commission we'd each receive for bringing home the bacon. And secondly if J.T found out about this dastardly plan we would expose ourself to a whole shit load of trouble in the form of an extremely vengeful J.T.

We ordered more beer and Al started to explain what he had in mind. Herb Silver was an old friend of Al's, they had worked together for a major U.S stock brokerage firm some twenty five years previously. Al explained that Herb was very well connected in the stock game and felt sure he would be more than happy to supply us with product, in the form of Reg S stock. And some pretty good looking stock too. He also felt that we would be able to purchase this stock at twenty five cents on the dollar giving us a massive 75% profit on the money we raised. It's fair to say he had my attention. It only took a nanosecond to work out that if we pulled this off with our gift client and redirected his $200,000 we'd make a whopping $150,000 between us. My thirst was really developing now so we did the only thing we could under the circumstances and ordered more beer. The idea of having Herb as our stock provider opened up all sorts of possibilities but the most pressing of immediate issues still remained. Where would the gift send his money? We didn't have two weeks to set-up an off-shore company with associated banking. I needed to act immediately, all of my lead up to this point meant that if I started pissing around now with delay after delay I'd stand to lose credibility with the gift and more importantly he would potentially go off the boil and lose interest altogether. I had him just where I needed him and tomorrow morning had to be trigger day or the whole thing was going to be a non-event.

Al then informed me that his sister, who lived on the other side of the pond, had a business bank account in Canada that she had set up a while ago for some small venture that had never taken off. The account name sounded ambiguous enough and could easily have been the name of a clearing agent, escrow or business services firm. But would his sister be up for something like this? Al felt sure she would, she wasn't particularly well off and if offered 2.5% of the total amount she cleared she'd make $5000. Money for old rope it seemed. All sorts of thoughts started whizzing through my head, not least that if all went according to plan Al and I would make a cool $72,500 each from this deal after paying for the stock and paying Al's sister for the privilege of using her bank account. Slightly more than we'd both make as closers for J.T and Nad. We'd be cutting them out of the deal completely, going behind their backs and basically be taking a massive dump on them from a great height. I justified this with the thought that if J.T was stiffing Big Tony then he deserved it, especially as it was Tony who had gifted Al and I the gift in the first place.

By 8pm we were back at Al's attic apartment that overlooked Plaza Catalunya in the very centre of Barcelona, an incredible view. Armed with a couple of rum and cokes, and with a couple of thick steaks on the grill and sharing a nice bit of weed, we studied a list of companies of which Herb could provide the Reg S stock . Herb had come through and had emailed us a list of four or five companies he could supply us, with immediate effect. Sourcing stock, it appeared, would not be an issue.

Al called his sister while I flipped the steaks over, deep in thought. Listening with interest I watched Al pace around his impressive roof terrace explaining the opportunity to his sis. Within five minutes I was wearing a massive grin as he winked and gave me the thumbs up. She was on board. We spent the remainder of the evening putting together a super-sexy story as to the potential ofthe stock we'd decided I'd pitch to the gift as well as preparing the necessary documents. When clients agree to a trade three documents are emailed to the client. Terms and conditions, the trade confirmation, and bank wiring instructions. The gift however preferred to be faxed these documents. This was perfect for me in this instance. I already had copies of trade documents in my inbox as I'd requested them a while back from one of the admin girls in order to refer to them when talking a client through the finer points should it become necessary. All I had to do was doctor them, print them off and I was off to the races. I'd just slip them into the office fax machine. The gift, if he bothered to look would see that the fax came from the usual number and company so no suspicions would be raised there. It would be much easier for me than having to hijack one of the admin girls' computers and start attaching my own cheeky little files.

By 1am I had all my doctored documents to hand and felt completely comfortable with the pitch I intended delivering to the gift. The die was cast. I was going in.

The following day the office was only half full. The admin girls were in, J.T and Nad were in and out but spending most of their time down the road in Fat Albi's air raid shelter. No other closers or fronters were in, J.T had given them the day off while he sorted things out. The office was very quiet, a perfect storm. I closed the sliding doors to our private office and made the call.

Unlike a new client, the gift didn't need to be overly sold on the company I were promoting, we had long passed that stage. It was all down to my enthusiasm and pitch as to the potential gains and the certainty of those gains becoming a reality that I so convincingly delivered. Basically I gave him both barrels leaving him in no uncertain terms and completely under the ether. After delivering my instructive closing question I shut up and waited. I'm a firm believer in the old adage, 'he who speaks first loses'. He spoke first.

Perhaps Al and I should have parted company with J.T and Nad right there and then. The gift however had always been a perfect client. He never called into the office, never sent faxes or emails and had no communication with the firm unless Al or I called him. Provided we kept him in the loop and rang him periodically there was no reason to fear he'd call in and it would all get exposed. So we didn't part company. We continued along the previously laid out plans of my taking over the Rambla Catalunya office and Al loading for both offices.

Later that afternoon I met with Jeff Rogers at the usual haunt and after a cold one we headed up to Albert Marvin's office to meet J.T and Nad. It was more or less a formality and we left the meeting within an hour, the keys to the Rambla Catalunya office safely in my pocket. It was a clear spring day, the air fresh and the sky blue and I felt excitement and massive potential in the very air around me. I'd just closed a deal that was worth $72,500 to me personallyand had also picked up the keys to my own show.

I've not been pulling any punches so let's keep it real as to the selfish motivations that drove me during this period of my life. It was all about me having a good time which translated to spending money in the best restaurants, drinking the best wine, getting high and bedding the most ridiculously gorgeous women. Let's call a spade a spade, I was a complete hound dog without a second thought for others during the years in which this story takes place, dating fabulous women and having more than my fair share of one night stands was what my life revolved around.

Barcelona is a hugely cosmopolitan city and within my stable of girls I had at one time or another, Brazilians, a Costa Rican, a Ukrainian, a couple of Russians, a Chinese girl, an Italian, a Filipino and of course the odd Spanish lovely, dare I say, to name a few. Juggling the stable was often fraught with danger as well as being a fairly expensive pastime. But hey, I had one hell of a time. I also woke with one hell of a headache the morning after the night before when I'd closed the gift and the office deal, a double whammy. Thank God it was a Saturday and I wasn't expected anywhere. I groggily made my way from the bedroom into my bright sunny lounge, way too bright on this morning. I stopped in my tracks as I cast my gaze over the wall behind my new, expensive Italian leather sofa. "What the..” I thought as I viewed the sweeping black marks on my ivory coloured wall. It looked like someone had used a black crayon and swished backwards and forwards for whatever reason I couldn’t imagine. Not coming up with any answers I got bored staring at it and headed for the Alka Seltzer and whatever else I could find that may help my current condition; coffee, scrambled eggs, ibuprofen and, and then it came to me. I smiled causing lightning bolts of pain to shoot through my temples. I’d cut one from the herd on my travels the previous night, an attractive primary school teacher from London on a hen night. Ironically the theme of the hen night had been naughty school girls and the gang were all suspendered, short skirted and tight topped. The black marks on my wall had come from the black high heels the gang had worn too, not all of them obviously, just the one who’d ventured into my den of iniquity throwing her legs in the air like she just didn’t care. Fortunately for me the marks sponged off the wall and there was no further action necessary. I was happily reminiscing in the kitchen when I heard the toilet flush and the shower being turned on. Fuck, she was still here. In fairness, she'd taken her clothes and bag with her to the bathroom not intending to wake me and to leave unannounced. When she appeared from the bathroom still dressed as she had been the night before it was impossible to say no. Besides I've always found hangover sex awesome.

She eventually left to meet her friends and continue with her hen party weekend of more shenanigans no doubt. Bless her. I never did find out who the actual hen was. It couldn't have been her, could it?

I met Jeff at the Aribau office mid-afternoon, I'd been given a set of keys as I had all my stuff to move. I also wanted Jeff to see the set-up that I intended to recreate in Rambla Catalunya, the sales figures being displayed for all and sundry to see on leader boards bolted to the walls. I also wanted to move various bits and bobs over; sales forms, scripts, call lists and the like. And last but not least I wanted to go through everyone's files with a fine tooth comb and steal as much information as I could concerning other clients' details. If Iwas going to do this I certainly wasn't going to be taking any prisoners.

Just over a year had passed since I'd arrived in the Catalan Capital. That era was coming to an end and a new one was about to begin. A much wilder and crazier era with events transpiring I never would have imagined but were just around the corner. Let the games begin.

Rambla Catalunya

"You, you fuck are a lazy useless piece of shit" I bellowed into the phone. "You're a fucking cunt" I added for good luck as I slammed my fist down onto my desk. "You need to get your fucking arse in here right now and we need to talk". I was ever so slightly peeved, and think I probably finished off with another "you cunt" before banging down the receiver. It was a Saturday morning, 11am, and I had arranged for all of my phone pirates to be in by 9am to smash the phones for a couple of hours, and two hours after we were all due to be revving up, no one was there. We did this occasionally to reach the difficult to contact prospects and it always brought positive results. I'd show up with doughnuts and coffee for everyone to start the blast off on the right foot, but this morning the coffee stood cold and the doughnuts just looked grumpy.

Business was going well, my pal Al was spending more and more time at my office and we were all writing plenty off business. Inevitably we were sending a large proportion of it to Al's sister's account thereby cutting J.T and company out of the deal completely. Those redirected funds securing 75% profit as opposed to the 40% going the J.T route. I'd personally bagged more than $150,000 for myself in the past two months I'd been in business with Jeff. And it was Jeff I'd given both barrels to this morning. I'd been calling his cell phone since 9.30am, he eventually answered at 11.00am. It transpired that he'd been out with the whole crew the night before and leading every single one of the idiots on a cocaine fuelled non-stop bender. They were all now camped out at Jeff's apartment still snorting the Colombian marching powder. To top it all off Jeff didn't seem to think it was a big deal and even invited me over to join in on the jolly.

Jeff was thirty four years old but looked about ninety when he appeared in the office less than an hour later wearing a huge pair of sun glasses and not particularly sure of his footing. I let rip as soon as he appeared calling him all the cunts under the sun. I gave him no chance to respond, defend himself, turn round or take a shit. I wanted to tear his arms off and beat him about the head with the soggy ends. I was fucking fuming. We had this huge opportunity and two months in Jeff had messed up big time, and not for the first time either.

I'd worked in sales rooms throughout Asia where you'd be told to go home and be fined $300 if you were so much a minute late in the morning. There'd be a sign on the locked door informing you. Make a habit of it and you'd be on a plane before you knew it. I'd worked at gigs where I've seen a guy in utter agony with toothache on a Wednesday and being told an appointment had been made for him for the weekend, given a shot of super strength pain killers, and told to get back on the phone. I'd seen an experienced closer ceremoniously removed from the office by security, escorted to the airport via his apartment to grab his shit quicker than he could say "what the fuck" all because he had talked negatively about the stock we were promoting. And the worst thing about all this is Jeff had seem all this and more as well.

Running a successful gig like ours took massive discipline, take your foot off the gas for a split second and the whole thing starts to crumble. Jeff needed to be leading by a different kind of example. There were no if ands of buts, not only did I intend to run a tight ship, I ran a tight ship. And if any of my pirates didn't like it then they could walk the plank. I'd made a promise to myself from the start of this journey that I wouldn't put up with any shit and would deal with it brutally. This wasn't breaking news, Jeff knew this. Working hard and playing hard was something I endorsed and absolutely encouraged. I'd taken the whole crew to an el clasico (football match between Real Madrid and Barcelona FC) followed by VIP at one of the city's most exclusive night clubs amongst other jollies as a reward for hard work and results, but here was my so-called business partner making a complete tit of himself in front of the people we were meant to be leading. Harsh as it may sound but I wasn't going to tolerate this. If I was seen to do nothing it would be seen as a sign of weakness and the slightest chink in the armour can have the same result as a laser guided missile. It'll fucking ruin you.

I demoted Jeff on the spot. He started to protest but my mind was made up. Many thought I was being unreasonable, but the fact of the matter is that no one took advantage after that. Not if they intended to keep their spot.

I made Jeff a closer but gave him a separate desk at the head of the sales floor and additionally the status of team leader. He'd get a couple of percentage points on the room's business as well as commission on his own business and loaded deals. Basically he was back on the main deck with the other pirates. As far as our partnership was concerned, that ship had sailed. In defence of my actions it had not been the first time Jeff had been AWOL. I'd had to go to his apartment twice of a morning within the last two months to get him up as he'd been on the blow all night. I'd warned him both times that I wasn't playing at this and if his habit continued to interfere with business then all bets were off. So I hadn't been a complete asshole.

Fate, destiny, the natural order of things or whatever you'd like to call it seemed to be at play. Al was spending more and more time at my office and by now had parked himself at the empty desk next to mine vacated by Jeff. We were putting more and more business through the sister's account so it made sense for us to occupy an office together in which to conspire. It was only a matter of time before we'd make this unofficial business partnership official. J.T was beginning to question the low levels of business my office was seemingly producing. It was producing plenty just not going through J.T.

I didn't want any hard feeling between Jeff and I so I took him to lunch a few days later to explain in a less furious manner that he'd left me with no alternative. He seemed resigned to the fact that it was inevitable and said he was happy not to have the responsibility and could now just concentrate and crack on with his own deals. It seemed he was happier writing business rather than running one. I still couldn't help wondering however, how long would he stick around? Sure, he would still make a bucket load of money but he'd still be aware of how much I was making and perhaps that little voice in his head would start chipping away telling him how hard done by he'd been. I made a mental not to work on other avenues of recruitment.

Spending money was not something I was shy about. I'm not saying it's clever but in this business it seemed that the super-consistent deal writers who'd bang in deal after deal day after day were also spendaholics. Perhaps it was the shock of realising how much money had been spent while glancing over a bank statement, or the fear of not being able to have it large the following month that drove me to perform, I can't say, but what I can say is that I wasn't going to let anything or anyone interfere with that. So if Jeff did decide to do one and bugger off with people he'd brought to the gig then I was going to be ready. I'm a great believer in the saying 'it's always better to cut them off at the pass'.

We all loved spending money, Al, me, Jeff, all of us, it's just that in Jeff's case too much of it went up his nose and then in turn he'd end up blowing thousands in a night camped out in a whore house. On more than one occasion I'd had to bail him out as he was being held hostage in a brothel having run out of cash and losing his bank card. Fortunately for me my drug of choice was weed and unlike coke it didn't turn me into an irrational sex fiend, but made me happy, hungry and healthily horny. Anyway, back to spending money and toys.

On a bright beautiful Barcelona Friday morning I mentioned to Al as we sat in our bosses office that I wouldn't mind buying a motor scooter to blast around the city. It was a hugely popular mode of transport and looked like a lot of fun. There were some pretty cool scooters out there too. The room was already buzzing so we excused ourselves and slipped out. Al was up for this as well and said it had been on his mind for a while. In fact no sooner had I mentioned it I think he was half way out of his seat telling me “let’s go pick up a couple”.

The Japs make great scooters but in Barcelona the Italian Piaggio is the scooter to be seen on if you’re in the know. Off we trotted to the main Piaggio dealership and within an hour of meeting Feran, the sales manager, we’d done all the paperwork and paid for two gleaming black Piaggio 250cc James Bond looking brand new scooters. At almost five thousand euros a pop they were reasonably priced for our spending habits but we still had more in the tank on this wonderful Friday. Or perhaps we were like sharks and had smelled blood and were now in a feeding frenzy to spend. We’d pick up the scooters the following Tuesday but we needed something tangible right now. So understandably as we passed the Rolex shop on Avinguda Diagonal, one of Barcelona's most elegant streets we popped in to pick up a couple of kettles. Al chose a two tone gold and stainless steel number, while I went for a stainless Sea-Dweller. Understated but class.

In high spirits leaving the store I literally walked straight into what I can only describe as a Goddess. As it turns out she was a Brazilian Goddess. "Oops, I'm sorry… oh, hello" I said, unable not to break into a huge smile. She wore a tight black t-shirt with the word Gucci emblazoned in small diamanté across her perfectly perky yet unsupported, breasts. Her figure hugging jeans and heeled sandals, classy jewellery and yep, a Rolex watch were all stood directly in front of me, and praise the Lord, she was returning my smile. Her hair looked like she should be doing T.V commercials for shampoo and conditioner. She wore her Gucci sunglasses atop her head which might as well have been a tiara. She spoke, "buenos dias". Al correctly read the situation saying, "I'll see you back at the office Champ" and buggered off accordingly. I'm not afraid of eye contact but her dark eyes had me transfixed, I couldn't steel myself away from her gaze – perhaps a Goddess trick. Her name was Herculana, or Lana for short and she was fabulous. Twenty eight and working in public relations. She declined my offer of lunch but gave up her phone number saying that maybe we could go for dinner sometime. We'd chatted for less than ten minutes but I'd already made up my mind that I'd do everything in my power to conquer Miss Brazil.

Back at the office spirits were exceptionally high. The guys were having a productive day and it was Friday in this amazing city. I took my twelve phone pirates to Café 7 after work on Fridays spending a couple of hours and a few hundred euros on drinks for my gang. This had quickly become a weekly ritual, enjoyed by all tremendously.

In the bosses office I shot the shit with Al concerning the obvious; our new scooters, new watches and what a fine piece of ass the Brazilian was. But the working day wasn't quite over yet. A week previously Al had loaded a Swiss banker based out of London for £50,000. His money had landed in Al's sister's account so it was time for me to go back in. Some clients had a way of surprising me and top of that list was this guy, Bo Hassler. The closer who had opened the account was a British Pakistani who went by the phone name of Chris Parker. Middle class Europeans were more likely to buy from a Chris Parker than an Ahmed Patel. Ahmed had relayed the story of the close saying that Bo had said nothing but grunt the occasional 'uh huh' throughout the pitch. Ahmed/Chris explained to Bo at the end of the pitch that as a first trade we set a cap of $15,000 for our private clients. The reason for this was nothing more than a client was far more likely to pay if it was a relatively small trade.

The bigger the initial trade the more likely the client would get cold feet and back out. Ahmed went on to explain to us that when he'd asked his final closing question and shut up that there'd been an unusually long silence, but Ahmed had stuck to his guns and refused to speak first. After perhaps thirty seconds of this stand-off and with his gruff heavily accented voice Bo announced, " zee stock is a dog. Put me down for zee maximum". So that's what Ahmed did, and good old Bo paid immediately.

Soon after Al had loaded the guy for $50,000. Again at the close he had remained silent for maybe thirty seconds before announcing " zee stock is still a dog. Put me down for zee fifty". And again, he paid just like that.

I still didn't really know Bo's ability. He'd been like the proverbial stone that you couldn't get blood from when it came to his volunteering of information so I decided to go in with a different strategy. I called Bo and introduced myself as the personal assistant to the great Al Parker. Incidentally the fact that Al Parker my business partner had the same surname as one of our closers Chris Parker was purely coincidental. Ahmed had chosen his Anglo Saxon name at a previous place that he'd worked at and didn't want to change his lucky name. No big deal. In the real world you don't go round telling people to change their names just because there's two of you that work in the same joint.

So here I was waiting to speak to this wonderful client Mr. Bo Hassler, for a wicked moment I thought of introducing myself as Fred Parker just for a laugh but Bo probably wouldn't have batted an eyelid and undoubtedly the joke would have fallen flat. So I didn't do that. I did this instead. I explained to Bo that I was making tentative enquiries on behalf of Al Parker regarding three blocks of drop-off stock, a term I'd just made up. This drop-off stock had just become available. I explained that the $50,000 trade he'd just completed had been part of an institutional allocation that Al controlled and distributed amongst our existing clients. As he knew, and I recapped, this institutional allocation due to our buying power had been purchased at 5% below the market price and in turn we were passing this discount onto our clients. Naturally this had been received well by all and the allocation had been a resounding success. Every word a fantasy. I went on to explain that the allocation had sold out on the first day we'd released it and consequently because of some unforeseen circumstances amongst a handful of clients we now had a limited amount of drop-off stock. In other words some clients had committed to fulfilling the trade but had had to back out. I further explained to Bo that one client for example, a South African, was unable to fulfil his trade because it had transpired that he owed the

South African government a relatively small back-tax, and the law being what it was in South Africa meant that this client could not transfer any funds outside the country until this oversight had been rectified. I had no idea if this was the case in South Africa but Bo didn't challenge me on it anyhow. Unfortunately for said South African dude it would be a couple of weeks before this tax crap was all sorted out and he was able to send funds. Again unfortunately for him, we couldn't wait that long. Poor guy was sick as a parrot that he was going to miss such a phenomenal opportunity. His stock, and two other clients stock had now become available for sale, as in drop-off stock. I told Bo to grab a pen and make a note of the values of these three blocks of stock. Bo wrote down the three values I dictated: $47,500, $82,750 and $150,000 exactly.

I then asked Bo which block he would be interested in before shutting the fuck up. I expected a long wait like the Parker boys had experienced but very quickly Bo shot me a question, “can I get zem all?”

I have to admit, old Bo did catch me by surprise, a little flat footed so to speak. In the ring that would have been classed as a sucker punch and I’d have been down for a eight count. We weren’t in the ring though, we were in my territory and I rolled with it. I calmly responded by saying that as far as I understood it was first come first served as we needed to complete the allocation, so yes. And that was that, the drop-off story was born with these three figures I’d plucked out of thin air at random. Three figures that totalled over $280,000. It might sound like pure fantasy but Bo’s money was as real as the day is long, and it was only mid-afternoon.

It had been a great week in more ways than one, Al was on form telling one of his fantastic tales as we all sat outside Café 7 in the late afternoon sunshine. It was a pretty funny story and the guys were loving it, hanging on every twist and turn as he spun his yarn in all sorts of unexpected directions with all sorts of characters with all sorts of unusual natures involved as it built to its climax – something to do with a dwarf and a Russian mafia don. But who really cares. I was enjoying the early drinks and the guys company but was only half listening to Al's supposedly true story as I was battling internally with my patience, or rather my lack of it. I consider myself an individual living in the now, living for the moment, and waiting patiently has never really been my thing. If I can do something now then why wait. Tomorrow is promised to none of us. In this instance my battle with patience involved one beautiful Brazilian. I totally understand the concept of not seeming over eager and showing my hand too soon. But equally, I understand the concept of striking while the iron is hot. I guess it's a case of horses for courses. And to use another analogy I suppose I was feeling as eager as a lion with his sights set on one of those springy little cute things. Gazelles? I felt dizzy at the thought of bringing the Brazilian down and feeding on her meat. I know I sound like a complete predator but the fact of the matter was that the girls I chased seemed to love being chased and once I'd caught them seemed to love hanging out with me. I'm just saying.

As anticipated my eagerness overrode my patience and I couldn't stop myself taking some affirmative action regarding the South American beauty. So I did what any brave, imaginative, red-blooded playboy would do. I sent her a text message. " Hi, it was nice to meet you today". Yep, corny and weak as hell, but right at that moment I couldn't think of anything cool and interesting to say, I just needed to release the gasket on my built up impatience. After about twenty minutes of obsessively checking my phone I decided I'd probably blown it with my sad-ass message. Regardless, as a drug addict feels temporarily satisfied after his hit, I felt satisfied I'd at least fired a shot across her bow and continued enthusiastically socialising with the crew. That said, I always paced myself in the company of the guys. I'd slaughtered Jeff for sinking to the depths he had and dragging the whole office down with him and there was never any danger of me getting completely out of control in the presence of my phone pirates.

By 8.30pm Al and I paid the tab, dropped another oner behind the bar and cabbed it back to Casa Parker for a rum or three on his spectacular roof-top terrace and to puff on a bone or two while watching the city's vibe change below as night replaced day.

Penka, Al's Bulgarian recently moved in girlfriend was there to meet and greet us with a smile when we arrived. Thirty years old and a keeper. Al had been chasing her for a while when she managed a popular bar in the city just off Las Ramblas. Yes, unbelievable but true, we did visit other drinking holes aside from Café 7.

Al twisted up our second bone and we were soon puffing on some mellow bud. Penka, true to her hospitality background brought us more pirate juice, Rum and Coke on the rocks, before retiring back inside the apartment leaving us boys to talk shop. Or more precisely at this time on a Friday night, to talk shit, a favourite pastime for both of us. Content and happy and high on life (weed and booze too) is how I felt during the many sessions we shared on that roof terrace. Forty minutes or so after we'd settled in something happened that trumped all of the day's activities. Something better than having bought a brand new super cool scooter. Better than my new Sea-Dweller that now adorned my left wrist, and even better than closing old Bo earlier that afternoon. In fact, something infinitely better than all of those things collectively. I received a text message from you-know-who. It read “nice 2 meet u 2 wot u doin?” Awesome! This was more than awesome, this was a fantastic development, trump of all trumps and praise the Lord. Now came the fun part, the game was on. I had the added enjoyment of having Al as an observer and sounding board for my next moves. But first we needed to top up on the performance enhancing drugs and pirate juice. My partner in crime called into the apartment to his Bulgarian Princess to do the honours. Another bone was twisted and I along with my two supporters, as Penka had now joined the party, went to work analysing Miss Brazil’s message and composing a suitable response. The second part of her message was key, “wot u doin?”. After a few puffs on the newly twisted bone and a healthy slug of rum to increase my thinking outside the box power, I believed I’d cracked it. “Wot u doin?” actually meant “wot u doin? If u r not bz do u wanna do sumfin?" Hmm interesting, but just as in big game fishing it's unwise to strike at the first nibble, it's much wiser to give a little more line, let her really take the bait then, Bam!

It was time to send my reply to this highly technical question, "wot u doin?". The first words I tapped out I quickly cancelled, "just left the office and was thinking of picking up some sushi, you?" Way too lame, she'd just told me she wasn't doing anything by the very fact she'd just asked me what I was doing. If she was out having fun she wouldn't have given a flying fuck about what I was doing, right? My response to her needed to be a little better than that first crappy effort. I ran my idea past Al and Penka and got the thumbs up. If I got the response I was angling for the deal would be in the bag. I tapped away and pressed send, "wondering if you liked sushi?".

It was a loaded question I hadn't met a beautiful girl who didn't like sushi. It was tasty, trendy healthy and sexy, what wasn't to like? And as luck would have it, I knew some of the best sushi restaurants around. Managers and staff at several knowing my name and giving me the VIP welcome which never hurts when you're out to impress.

My tail was up, I was feeling good, confident and ready to gamble, so I hit up my phone book and dialled Parco, one of Barcelona's premier sushi restaurants located on Passeig de Gracia, just above Diagonal where I'd earlier bumped into Lana after buying my new watch. Parco, a trendy contemporary spot has a great atmosphere, great music and of course exceptional sushi. It was owned and run by a Frenchman, Max, and you needed to be well informed to know about it. Word of mouth was how it ran. Many of the top eateries saw it as a mark of having achieved ultimate success when any form of traditional or paid marketing just wasn't needed. And Parco slots right into that category. If Lana accepted my soon-to-be invitation to dine with me tonight she'd be either impressed by my choice if she was familiar with this fabulous little gem, or equally impressed if strolling into the joint for the first time. I was betting the girl knew about Parco. Young, beautiful and looking like a million dollars, she'd told me she worked in P.R, so I felt it highly likely she was in the know. Max answered my call and although it was always fully booked he managed to squeeze me in for 11.30pm. Perfect. Nobody in Spain even thinks about sitting down to dinner before 9pm and many consider that to be way too on the early side. I thanked Max and hung up then noticed I had a message. My co-conspirators were just as eager to see if my cunning plan was falling into place. It was. The Brazillian's message read "mmm love it ;)". Mmm I fucking love it! Not a plain old ‘yep’ or ‘it’s nice’ but an mmmm I fucking love it, with a smiley face too, a fucking winking smiley face!

Al and the Bulgarian had winking smiley faces on themselves by now too, as they jokingly and happily watched events unfold. I immediately tapped into my phone “Parco 11.30pm?” And hit send. I calmly took a sip of rum, I knew this was in the bag and about to be check mate. Seconds later she hit me back, “I love Parco, see you there”. It was game on.

The date went perfectly, Lana looked stunning dressed for dinner in a figure hugging little black number that exposed plenty of delicious cleavage. It turned out she was incredibly susceptible to my secret weapons of seduction. Namely, listening intently when she spoke, encouraging her to elaborate, appearing impressed, amused and basically showing the called for responses at the correct times. And of course, making her laugh. I’ve always found that that combination used correctly can act as a tremendous aphrodisiac especially when deployed in such sumptuous surroundings. The exceptional wine didn't hurt either. Later that evening I was to discover that beneath that sexy little black number, Lana was clad in black and silver grey lingerie by Fredericks of Hollywood.

When we woke the following morning Lana was a little surprised she'd fallen asleep and stayed the whole night. Although she very quickly embraced the idea that it might be fun to hang around for a couple of hours and before long I was cooking breakfast for two. Morning seeped into afternoon and it was gone three o'clock before Lana reluctantly said she'd have to go. She seemed a little surprised that I didn't have a car and would therefore not be able to drive her home. Normally she would have enjoyed the walk but with heels and her evening garb on a scorching Barcelona summer afternoon she resigned herself to the fact it was going to be a taxi. "But you are boss" she said to me with her fabulous Brazilian accent, “you are businessman” she continued, “you should have car, you need car”. And thinking about it she was absolutely right. It seemed to me that if my real passion of being a philandering playboy was to reach it’s true potential then I needed a suitable chariot as a necessary tool of the trade.

Lana was ready to leave, when she came and sat next to me on the sofa, taking my hands in hers and looking solemnly into my eyes. She looked pretty upset, like she had the weight of the world on her shoulders – could she really be this upset about my lack of wheels? “Look, I’m sorry I don’t have a…” I started to say but was stopped in my tracks by her closing her eyes and shaking her pretty little head. “No, no it’s not that” she said “I don’t care about you don’t have car” OK, I thought, so why the grim look? “I like you” she said, I liked her too and told her as much, “maybe we can do this again?” which suited me down to the ground, "but I have to tell you something first". Shit, she'd better not used to have been a bloke, I thought. "I'm an escort" she said. Well I guess that's P.R, right? Holy fucking moly, the Brazilian beauty was a hooker, brilliant, I'd bagged myself a top shelf prozzy for free! I suddenly came to my senses and realised that maybe she wanted me to pay, she was just sat there looking at me with this kind of expectant expression on her lovely face. " Uh, do you want me to.." I was going to say pay but she anticipated my words and playfully slapped my leg, "no silly, it's not like that, that's my work and this is different". Brilliant, I thought for the second time, I really had bagged myself a top-notch high class hooker for free. If I could keep her as a friend with benefits she'd definitely be one to add to the stable. What a result I couldn't have been happier. A fabulous no strings attached relationship was on the cards with a beauty who I found out later could make €2000 for an overnight ‘girlfriend’ experience. I was keen to hear about her work and the different stories she must have to tell but I didn’t want to appear too elated by this fabulous revelation that she was a hooker, especially as her demeanour seemed to indicate that I should be looking a little sad, or upset or something along those lines, and not like I did with a big Cheshire Cat grin plastered across my face. “I do have an open mind” I said “and I understand it’s just work” I went on “and I’ve enjoyed being with you too, it was fun and if you want to do it again we can”. She left happy in the knowledge we’d hook up again and that I had taken her revelation in my stride and she had especially seemed to perk up when I told her that next time we meet I might even have a car.

I saw Lana on and off for the next three years , she was an excellent addition to the stable and as it happens turned out to be worth her weight in gold. I never got tired of the buzz I got when she'd turn up at my place bearing gifts. Guys were paying thousands for the pleasure of her company - one guy paid her €5000 to accompany him on a three day trip out to Mallorca – and here she was showing up to hang out with yours truly and now and again bringing me a new shirt or whatnot.

After Lana left that afternoon I set to work finding a suitable car. The following Wednesday I transferred €60,000 euros in exchange for a gleaming black Porsche 911 Carrera. A fair bit of dosh I know, but somebody was going to pay for it and it certainly wasn't going to be me.

That week I decided two things. Firstly I'd make Al an equal partner and secondly I'd cut J.T out of the loop completely. They were profitable decisions. Within four weeks I'd replaced the money I'd spent on my new fanny-magnet. I did have the unpleasant task however of breaking the news to J.T that it was goodnight Vienna as far as our business relationship was concerned. J.T wasn't stupid and had suspected something was up for a while, there was no way we were only doing the amount of business that we were putting through him with the talent I had in my room. I made the call and in true non-beating about the bush fashion laid it on the line. "I knew it.." was followed by a whole bunch of insults and threats. When on the receiving end of such a tirade I always find it best to do the shutting the fuck up thing and let the guy going nuts burn himself out. "Perhaps we should meet" I finally said once J.T had run out of things to say, worn himself out or just got plain tired of dumping on me. We met at Café Zurich on Plaza Catalunya just opposite Hard Rock Café. He appeared calm. The gist of our meeting was that he wanted me to compensate him for the office fixtures and fittings including desks, chairs, phone system, photocopier, fax, T.V's, cabinets and all that sort of crap. I felt he was being rather petty if I'm being honest but I guess it was the only thing he felt he could do. Fair enough I thought and agreed on €20,000. The meeting was over although I doubted this is the last I'd see of J.T. I met with Al at Café 7 after J.T and I parted company and celebrated the day's events with a cold one and a pre-twisted bone that appeared as if by magic from Al's sleeve. I have to admit, it felt great to have cut free from J.T and Nad. I was hugely appreciative of the opportunity I'd found in Barcelona but once Big Tony left the party and I'd seen how J.T had stiffed him any loyalty I'd felt to the group went up in a puff of smoke. I don't regret any of my underhandedness toward J.T and found out years later that he'd subsequently gone on to rip off Nad's parents for $100,000. I don't know the details but the words came directly from Nad's mouth. Like I said, I was a relieved to have cut loose and was filled with a wild excitement at the possibilities that stretched out in front of me.

Al and I were now in complete control and all our business would go through Herb Silver giving us maximum returns on all monies we raised. Herb continued to give us great looking deals, often with regular press releases concerning the companies we were promoting, hugely favourable press releases across various main stream news wires, thus providing us with even more credible reason to go back into clients to extract even more. If we did nothing else we hit them hard. Additionally because many of these companies had such low volumes (not a lot of stock being bought on the open market), and in some cases no volumes at all, it was easy for Herb to manipulate the price by instigating a few small trades. Again, any small movement would have us banging the phones again aggressively encouraging clients to up the ante on their existing holdings. Of course it was wrong. It was rotten, deceitful, and underhanded. We were in the greed business. We were driven by greed and it was that that drove many of our clients into believing stories that were too good to be true. And I'm not for one moment justifying my actions during those years that saw investors lose millions and millions of dollars, no, not at all. I do however want to point out that far bigger and far reaching frauds are carried out by seemingly honourable organisations right under our noses every single day. And what's even more disturbing is that many individuals known to the authorities, in fact captains of industry go completely unpunished. To highlight this point here are several extracts from an August 2014 USA Today article entitled Largest U.S Corporate Penalty – Yet No Villains:

'Bank of America's $16.5 Billion Settlement with The Department of Justice over selling toxic mortgage securities in the years before the Nation's financial crisis is the largest in history for an individual company'. Hmm serves 'em right,

right? And how about this snippet 'No present or former bank officials were identified as responsible' Well I guess it must have just happened on its own then. 'No details on investor losses or bank gains'. Again, hmm. And here's one I particularly like. 'How many tens of millions of dollars did bank of America's customers, clients, investors and others lose due to years of knowing, systematic fraud? How much did Bank of America make from its illegal actions? Asks Dennis Keller, president and CEO of Financial Watchdog Better Markets' So, if it's knowing and systematic how come no present or former bank officials were identified? Strange. Especially when, 'much of the activity covered by the settlement occurred in Countrywide Financial, the mortgage company the bank bought in 2008, and Merrill Lynch, the brokerage the bank also acquired during the financial crisis' it gets worse, 'Merrill Lynch and Countrywide Financial sold billions of dollars of

RMBS (residential mortgage backed securities) backed by toxic loans whose quality and level of risk they knowingly misrepresented to investors'. Then the Attorney General at the time jumps in. 'Attorney General Eric Holder said, these loans contained material underwriting defects: they were secured by properties with inflated appraisals; they failed to comply with federal and state laws; and they were insufficiently collateralized. Yet these financial institutions knowingly, routinely, falsely and fraudulently marketed and sold these loans as sound and reliable investments'. So all I'm really saying is if the Attorney General, the top lawyer in the country, can make these claims how the fuck was nobody identified as responsible. I'm just saying.

Back to Rambla Catalunya and the goings on there. Al and I were about to face the first of our logistical challenges. The day J.T received the funds for all the office crap he visited our office together with Nad and Albert Marvin. It was left to Fat Albi to deliver the news. The office lease was in his name and because of his ongoing business relationship with J.T and Nad and in view of our recent parting of ways, he felt it was a conflict of interest to allow us to continue to sublet the office from him and consequently must ask us to vacate sharpish. Fat poof. J.T sat silently with rather too much of a smug look on his face for my liking. Fat poof Albert Marvin went on to say that by sharpish he meant 48 hours. My initial thought was to tell them to go fuck themselves and throw them down the stairs, but Al sensing my conflict levels rising saved a physical confrontation from erupting by asking the three of them to leave and we'd contact them by the end of the day. J.T decided it was time for his two pennies worth and voiced his opinion that we had no choice in the matter, he went on to blurt something out about being well connected and was generally acting like a little bitch. I felt like I was seconds away from launching myself at him and beating him half to death with my desk phone when Al bellowed "out!" At the top of his lungs while at the same time pointing at the door. Our crew heard the eruption and were now all staring in through our large window that overlooked the sales floor. They had senses something might go down and on hearing Al's thunderous roar had one by one ended their calls and started moving in. The three assholes saw the gradual approach of some fairly hefty phone pirates so decided it best to comply with Al's order. I moved to our office door and opened it so the three could leave, at the same time letting the guys know it was OK and that our guests were leaving. As they shuffled out Fat Albi said he didn't want any problems which made sense but at the same time I knew J.T was not the type to let this go. After they'd left it didn't take long for me to see sense too. It was a crazy idea to dig our heels in and stay, we'd be jeopardizing everything, we were making more money than ever before and for the sake of pride and ego we'd potentially lose it all by remaining put in Rambla Catalunya. We'd be sitting ducks for whatever J.T decided to send our way. We could of course fight back but it just wasn't worth it. We decided that afternoon that we'd move. The obvious short term solution was serviced office accommodation that would allow us to move in immediately and continue working without missing a beat. I also arranged immediately for the Rambla Catalunya office to be completely stripped. If J.T thought I was going to walk away from all the office crap I'd just paid for he was sadly mistaken. I thought about ripping the carpets up too but decided against it in the end.

Within 48 hours of our meeting with the three stooges we were settled temporarily in serviced offices based out of The World Trade Centre in the port area of the city.

The accommodation was not ideal but we'd succeeded in keeping the business running with hardly any down time. Mine and Al's priority now that we had the guys banging the phones again was to find our pirates a new home. I'd not realised how useful our scooters would be during this period as we tore around the city from one office viewing to another. In less than a week we found our new H.Q on Ronda San Pere, right next to the city's largest department store, El Cort Ingles. It was a fabulous spot. The office was perhaps a little on the large side for our current requirements but would encourage us to grow into it. While I was chatting to the real estate agent who was handling the lease, she mentioned the lease was available on a fantastic bachelor pad, an attic apartment in the building next door. "How do you know I'm a bachelor?" I asked smiling. She shrugged, smiled a naughty little smile back and just said "I don't. Do you want to see it?" Anna was kind of geeky looking but attractive nonetheless, she had a strange yet magnetic draw. I was intrigued to see this bachelor pad if it meant spending a little more time with this peculiar girl. I'm glad I did. I loved it. Everything was perfect. The kitchen, the bathroom, the open plan living area, the exposed beams, the solid oak polished flooring throughout, to the two terraces front and rear, both decked, one with a great canopy and dining area, the other with views to the Mediterranean complete with sun deck and outside shower. Everything was pure quality and according to Anna had been designed by one of Spain's top designers. True of otherwise I didn't care. I absolutely loved it. The idea of bringing my guests back here was making my heart race. It also came with underground parking, the lift bringing me right to my front door. Awesome I thought, a lady wouldn't have to walk at all on route back to my love shack. Exit Porsche, clip clop, enter den of iniquity. Fantastic, I loved it. Obviously I was going to take this place. I was staring toward The Mediterranean day dreaming when Anna interrupted my thoughts, “so what do you think?”. Turning to face Anna I realised she was not just attractive but beautiful behind her geekiness. “You know what” I said “I’m going to take it” and with my cheekiest smile, added “and was wondering if you liked sushi?”.

Ronda San Pere

It turns out that Anna was not actually called Anna. Nowhere near. Her real name was Natalia. What the hell, didn't anyone in this city use their real names? Lana's hooker name was Erica and now I was finding out my real estate agent was wandering around with a fake name too.

We were enjoying a very pleasant evening at Big Fish, another of Barcelona's great sushi restaurants located in the El Borne district, one of the city's oldest and dating back to Roman times. From here, this fantastically historic location, Barcelona had grown to the sprawling metropolis it is today. But enough of the history lesson, let's get on.

It was mine and Natalia's first date. The geek had basically turned into Cinderella. Not as designer labelled as Miss Brazil but an understated natural beauty. Cinderella she may have been but not the blonde haired blue eyed numbskull variety like in the cartoon. No, not one bit. Natalia hailed from Costa Rica, her mother a local of that beautiful country, her old man however had been a Jap. She was a perfect mix of Asian beauty and hot Latin lover. She had an understated confidence and independence I found incredibly attractive. Far wiser than her 23 years yet still maintained a playful youthfulness during the few years we remained close. Our relationship was not a natural match, but strangely enough was probably the most honest throughout my fooling around years in the Catalan capital.

Natalia had arrived in Barcelona not long before I had, but unlike me who basically arrived to inflict financial ruin on others, she was here to study photography. A two year course in one of Europe's finest visual arts schools. She was working the real estate angle to supplement the grant she'd won that financed the course and partial living costs. The fake name she was using wasn't so much fake, it just wasn't hers. One of the girls at the shared apartment where Natalia lived, a local, had allowed her to use her I.D in order she could work, as Natalia's visa was of the student variety that didn't qualify her to work. She was one of life's true free spirits, as cool as they come. I felt a genuine connection with her that first evening and unlike my first date with Lana where I had one goal in mind, I was interested in this girl. Her questions were forthright and unusual which was extremely refreshing and a pleasant change to the usual dinner talk that I'd found had become routine with most girls.

As we walked to my car while continuing our easygoing yet engaging conversation my mind suddenly entered the mode of 'what now?'. It had been a fantastic evening and I'd have liked nothing more to continue it back at the ranch, but didn't want to ruin it if that kind of suggestion would blow my chances of a second meeting. In the car I casually asked “home?”. Equally as casually and as quick as a cat she answered “mine or yours?” And flashed me a cheeky little smile. Shy and backward in coming forward is not something I can be accused of and that magical night with Natalia, the free-spirited Asian Latina beauty only got better from that point on.

During the next seven days Al and I pulled out all the stops to make sure our new office was ready to rock ‘n roll. Our goal had been to be fully installed, fully operational and firing on all four cylinders within seven days of taking possession. It was a tall order. New carpets, blinds, paint, artwork, T.V’s and a €30,000 state of the art phone system with all the latest features, including ‘barging’ that would allow me, Al, a manager or team leader to jump on a call and listen in. A great training tool being able to coach and give advice in real time.

To achieve this seven day goal in Spain where everything seems to be approached at a snail's pace was a tall order indeed. When a Spanish contractor tells you 'manana' it doesn't necessarily mean tomorrow. When he tells you 'si es posible', it basically means that the job in question is highly unlikely to happen tomorrow. And if you ever hear the words 'es posible proxi semana' (it's possible next week), it categorically means that there's not a snowballs chance in hell of it ever happening. That said, through our relentlessness and the odd bribe we did achieve our goal. In seven days we were done.

Allow me to harp on about our super-fandagled phone system for a moment. The added expense we went to in installing this weaponry, when I'd already ripped a perfectly functioning system out of the Rambla Catalunya office, over time proved to be completely justifiable. It was a prime example of feature function benefit. The benefits we enjoyed included the obvious of more business, but additionally the not so obvious. We started attracting pirates from other gigs in the city due to our reputation as a professional outfit that had it going on. All our phones for example had wireless Plantronics earpieces that enabled pirates to charge around the office while pitching and pillaging. This was great as most of the rooms in the city had their pirates tethered to their desks, and no one likes being tethered to a desk. Besides, motion creates emotion and in our type of high energy environment the constant movement created a fantastic buzz.

Our sudden forced departure from Rambla Catalunya had ultimately done us a great favour in elevating our business to the next level and been a great test of our resilience. A test that we came through with flying colours. From successful closers we'd stepped up to the plate and proved we were a force to be reckoned with in this dastardly game. If J.T's intention had been to bury us he'd done exactly the opposite and shown us to be worthy business owners.

A term I grew very fond of during these years was 'let's cut them off at the pass'. When suspecting something or someone is going against me I've always found that to 'cut them off at the pass' pays dividends. Let's form a posse and cut them off at the pass. Love it. Another great one if something was bothering me was 'why take a chance?'. In fact the two usually went hand in hand. "Why take a chance, let's cut them off at the pass"

My immediate goal once we'd achieved our 'seven days to get rock n rolling' target was recruitment. Not only was the new office too large for our current needs, I was aware that Jeff would now see me and Al as true bosses and that would be bound to rub him the wrong way which was completely understandable. It was only a matter of time before he upped sticks and skedaddled, taking a few of the guys with him he'd brought in the first place. So why take a chance? I wasn't going to be caught flat footed so needed to act fast just in case.

I'd known a guy by the name of Graham Walsh when I'd first arrived in Barca, and had actually first met him at a gig in Cyprus several years previously. He'd been around the business since the late nineties and always left a string of wild stories in his wake. A Northerner, a larger than life character and very likeable but with a dark side when on the ale. He'd had to leave Barcelona in a hurry not long after I'd arrived due to the fact he clobbered a cop. Not the great decision he ever made. Graham had recently set himself up as the go to guy for recruiting new pirates. Smart, as there was a gap in the market that he would now fill. Boiler room operations are not the kind of business that seek staff through normal channels. Graham placed all sorts of ambiguous sounding advertisements in the national press that promised potentially very attractive on target earnings. He'd receive plenty of responses, meet the candidates and assess who he would be able to groom for these positions that were slightly off the beaten and somewhat off the straight and narrow as it happens as well. The service he provided was perfect for the many, many boiler room operations around the globe. With more than his fair share of front line experience Graham knew exactly what it took to succeed in this high-pressure, high-energy environment and so was perfectly placed to provide this much in demand service.

A new recruit cost €2000. A grand up front and another one after a four week probationary period. If we binned the new recruit before the four weeks expired we'd get a replacement free of charge, having only to pay the outstanding thousand euros.

He sent us some good pirates, but wasn't a magician so occasionally we'd get a dog or two. Two particular dogs I remember were two female dogs. Bitches I believe is the correct term. Rough as old boots they looked like they could probably fuck up half the lads in the office. They were completely useless, and like most people who couldn't cut the mustard, would blame everything and everybody else for their failings. It's a fact that women are few and far between that succeed in the male dominated boiler room environment. And with the exception of an extremely successful ex-glamour model who manned the decks of our pirate ship for a couple of years, I never met one. After four weeks of giving the dog girls every opportunity it became glaringly obvious that they were never going to sell stock as long as they had holes in their arses. They'd never crack it. I called them into my office to give them the 'good news'. Not a job I loved doing, made worse by the fact that getting rid of people meant we'd lost money, as we'd pay for flights, give all pirates -in -training €100 per week walking around money as well as put them up in one of our company apartments. And that's not to mention the leads they burnt and all the associated office costs. The two ugly sisters seemed to take it well and we said our goodbyes and good lucks. My secretary, a promising tennis player from Croatia went to let a cleaner into the apartment a few hours later. If you're wondering why I haven't been particularly kind when commenting on these two recently departed pieces of pond-life you'll understand now. My secretary called from the apartment, a nice two bedroom place in the Raval district that had been completely renovated before I took over the lease. These two English roses had completely trashed the place including amongst other things urinating and defecating on the beds as well as rubbing faeces on the walls, inside the kitchen cabinets and inside the refrigerator. There was shit everywhere, so it's completely accurate and appropriate to assume these two little tramps were completely full of it. No one left our employ after that without the apartment being checked over first. Newcomers passports were held to insure no repeat performance. I decided we really could do with a security guy to manage the apartments and take care of our people and any problems that might arise outside the office.

Paulo the security fella that had worked for Big Tony, the second person I'd met from the firm after landing on Spanish soil, was working for Nad, who was now running his own gig separate from J.T, but apparently not that happy there. He'd always respected me, so when I called him and told him I had a proposition that I thought he'd like, he couldn't have gotten to our office any quicker if those two shit-slinging slags had been chasing him with their crap covered hands. After an hour I basically made him an offer he couldn't refuse and voila, we had our security guy.

Once on board Paulo made it be known that two of the top closers from Nad's office could probably be tempted to jump ship and join us. So, Al, Paulo and I accidentally on purpose bumped into the pair in a local Spanish bar frequented regularly by said pair, called The Frankfurt. This traditional Spanish bar, there seemed to be one on every corner of every block, was run like most in the city, by Chinese. A Spanish bar called the Frankfurt run by Chinese. Yeah, I know.

Al and I are likeable characters who knew how to have a good time, and were particularly in our element amongst the city's drinking establishments. After Paulo had made the introductions it wasn't too long before we were knocking them back with the pair like best of buddies. It played out well, Paulo was selling the opportunity for us and was reeling these two proven closers in without Al or I having to really say much about the gig at all. I don't suppose it hurt either when Paulo started drooling over the fact that we had some real beauties working in the office. Three lovelies in administration and one ex-glamour model on the sales floor to be precise. Add to the mix these two guys were having a whale of a time with their prospective bosses who were quite obviously picking up the tab. I felt sure these two pirates would soon be landing on the decks of our good ship and a couple of days later Paulo got a call from the lads wanting to set up a meeting. Job done.

Graham had also sent us a couple of guys who were proving their worth. I always worked to build teams of fronters around guys that could close. The way to keep a quality closer is to feed him quality leads and I knew from my own personal experience in the trenches that to do that I needed to give him quality fronters.

The room was developing well, we had a mix of fronters and closers and guys that were developing into decent closers. With those guys I'd start them off closing their own fronts and if they proved their salt and I deemed them ready I'd allocate them a couple of fronters of their own. Closing with a team of fronters is where they could really start raking it in making upwards of €20,000 per month if they were any good, and sometimes a lot more than that. The whole show was performance based and we rewarded good performance well. During our reign of terror we ran plenty of incentives that saw winners wearing brand new Rolex watches, taking luxury vacations, and zooming off on Harley Davidsons, to name but a few.

My decision to proactively develop recruitment aggressively was well founded, as within months of parking ourselves in the Ronda San Pere office my old friend Jeff and four of his pals pissed off. It pissed me off that he hadn't announced his departure, but rather just 'did one', but only for a few minutes. It was what it was, I'd seen it coming and acted accordingly and ultimately I had a business to run, there was no time for sour grapes. I would have like to have wished him well and shook hands but life goes on. We now had an overspill of fronters for the remaining closers which translated into them getting more leads. Happy about this they closed more deals and I was extremely happy that at the end of that month the figures confirmed that we'd done more business the month of the mini exodus than we'd ever done before. By actively recruiting since moving in to our current location I'd cut off the threat while created a more productive machine .

Even so, we were still down five bodies and my focus was on filling the office. Empty desks were empty business centres, like vacant units in a shopping mall, it doesn't feel right and sends out the wrong message. Timing was everything however and my goal of filling the office was about to take a huge leap forward while bringing an unexpected cash infusion. Herb Silver, our stock provider, had associations with some very wealthy individuals, who, for one reason or another had access to large amounts of Reg S stock. Some owned the companies, others had acquired it in various dealings, but either way it owed them very little, so selling it for 25 cents on the dollar of the freely traded price was often pure profit for them. I suspect that in some circumstances the companies had been formed purely to create the Reg S stock, but the company as a viable entity was non-existent. I never actually knew this for sure, and if you saw the websites, business plans, directors' resumes, press releases and the fact that the companies were listed on the OTCBB or Pink Sheets and the fact that some of the CEO's would sometimes host tele-conferences for the benefit of investors informing them of the company's bright and sunny future, you'd be hard pressed to determine what was real and what wasn't as well.

Some of the companies were real however I knew for sure. I bought shares in a couple for my own benefit, although I bought the freely trading shares not the Reg S variety. Made some money too. In fact some of our investors did as well. We assisted them in getting the restriction lifted and they made over 100% profit in one instance. That was a rare occurrence however. Anyway, back to Herb Silver. He approached us about an associate of his, a very wealthy citizen of one of the United Arab Emirate countries who was keen to off-load a whole bunch of Reg S stock. Trouble was, we were doing well with our current deal. The guys on the phone were comfortable and familiar with it and things were hunky dory, so why change? There was no reason for us to ditch our current recommendation for something new. Or was there? I explained to Herb that we'd just lost some good guys and my focus was on filling the room and developing new guys, not dumping a new deal on my existing guys and having to spend unnecessary time with them getting them in the groove and banging in the deals again.

Everything has a price though and when Herb informed me that his associate would drop $100,000 on me and another $100,000 on Al, just to take the deal it started to make a lot more sense. To top it off, Herb, at his expense, would conduct a recruitment drive in the States and promised to send us between eight and ten guys and would even fly over for a couple of weeks to assist in their training. Happy days.

Herb and his associate stood to make a lot of money if we took their deal, but my partner and I would get a $100,000 cash infusion each and a truck load more pirates to boot. We took the deal. As it was we kept our current recommendation as well and ran with both opportunities, mixing and matching so to speak. The windfall came in handy for the purchase of a couple of new Harley's and a five star road trip to France that included stops in Saint Tropez, Monaco and Cannes, where we spent a fair chunk of change of fine wine, fine women and an evening at the casino surrounded by what seemed like a whole entourage of minor, and a few major movie stars. It was Cannes Film Festival, and the rich and famous had come out to play. It was a riotous trip and for the sake of protecting the identities of those involved I'll just say that what happens in Cannes stays in Cannes. One little known, at the time, aspiring actress, could have joined the circus as the incredible sword swallowing lady if the acting thing hadn't worked out. A memorable trip. Enough of reality, let's get back to the world of make believe – the office.

Over the next few weeks Herb, true to his word, recruited and sent us the new guys he'd promised, followed up with him visiting us to assist in training this new bunch of misfits.

Our reputation was growing favourably on the city's boiler room grapevine and we started attracting more phone pirates from other rooms. Sometimes this worked out but more often than not it was a case of the grass being greener on the other side. If they'd not made any money elsewhere then just because we had a fancy phone system, and a classy set-up it didn't translate to them all of a sudden becoming top closers. Likewise with the Americans that Herb recruited, the vast majority were pretty useless if the truth be known. Recruiting was an ongoing project, even though that within six months of Jeff leaving with four of our guys I'd built the room up to six competent, consistent closers with teams of between two and four fronters a piece.

The Arab was pleased with the amount of his stock we were selling and invited me and Al, along with Herb and Graham, our go-to recruitment guy, to Dubai for a meeting on an all-expenses paid weekend. He wanted to explore the possibility of us opening an office out there on his manor. We played along but never really had any intention of spreading ourselves too thin by expanding too quickly this early in our reign. It would have been a good ego boost but a bad business decision. Al and I planned to meet the others there and flew business class to Amsterdam and then from there on to Dubai on that first class airline, Emirates. Fly Emirates is their catch phrase and fly Emirates we certainly did, taking full advantage of the excellent on board cuisine and booze.

Our six star hotel was out of this world and had the benefit of a revolving bar plonked on the very top floor, miles up it seemed, with fantastic views across this Arabian landscape and sea. Graham was due to arrive from the UK later that evening with Herb touching down the following morning. So that afternoon Al and I had a wander around HD Mall of the Emirates and marvelled at its huge indoor ski-resort. Coming across a shop that sold the traditional middle eastern garb of the white robe, called the dishdasha and the red and white checked ghutra, or headscarf, that's secured with a black rope like cord, called the igal, we decided it would be fun to get a couple of sets. The nice man in the shop showed us how to fold the scarf and wear it and soon after, wearing sunglasses as well, we looked like a couple of regular oil sheiks.

That evening we'd arranged to meet Graham in the revolving bar. The views at night were equally impressive, the twinkling lights of outlying areas and a full bright moon made for a completely different, yet nonetheless magnificent viewing experience. Just for kicks, we wore out Arab disguises complete with sunglasses for added inconspicuousness. We were the only two in the exclusive bar dressed this way and looked like we could be a circus act, 'The Camal Jockey Brothers' perhaps. Most guys were dressed in business suits, the ladies in cocktail dresses. Although I felt like we were in fancy dress no one paid us any attention, maybe assuming we were the real deal. After thirty minutes or so and well into our second pirate juice, Graham sauntered in, scanning all around as he moved towards the bar and as I'd hoped not spotting us. "Gray" I called as he ordered himself a drink, no more than thirty feet from where we sat. Sniggering, I looked away and took another sip as Graham spun around none the wiser. I did this a few more times much to our great amusement before the head scratching Graham cottoned on. “Surprise” I called lowering my sunglasses and grinning at a now laughing Graham. It was the start of an excellent night. Not long after we’d stopped fucking around with Graham six members of the Emirates flight that brought us in that afternoon showed up. Needless to say we steamed in. Our Arab threads a tremendous ice breaker as well as a source of great amusement. We retold the Graham entering the bar story and within minutes it seemed we were all best mates. The crew consisted of five girls and one lad, all Dutch, and although I’d only recognised the two girls who’d served us in Business Class when they’d entered the bar I was soon getting on extremely well with a green eyed pixie who went by the name of Tess. Twenty seven years old, as fit as a fiddle with a wicked sense of humour. Tess was definitely my type of flight attendant. Although I much preferred calling her my air stewardess behind closed doors. As the evening wore on and our conversation grew saucier, it became pretty damn obvious to me that the classic one-night-stand was on the cards. And a little after midnight having stopped off at Tess's room for her to collect her uniform we were back in mine with her performing a risqué version of the pre-flight safety presentation, which I feel completely confident in saying has never been performed in front of a plane load of passengers. In exchange for this magnificent display I had promised to show Tess what an Arab gentleman wears under his dishdasha, which in my case by now was fuck all. A fantastic session ensued with this little pocket rocket which resumed at daylight as I woke to find her eyes staring up at me from my nether regions. A very nice way to start the day. Fly Emirates indeed.

Back in Barcelona and a little over a year since I'd severed ties with J.T we'd built the office to thirty phone pirates having rearranged the space to accommodate the numbers as initially it had been set up to comfortably accommodate twenty five. It was a good strategy to have the room feel busy, it created an awesome buzz that is obviously not found in rooms with an abundance of space and where phone pirates are rattling around. It makes a pirate feel too special, too needed. It sends the wrong message. I'd prefer to burn a desk rather that have it sit empty. I wanted people to feel privileged to have their spot.

The original boiler rooms, started by the mob back in twenties New York, operated out of boiler rooms in basements in the business district. These spaces were crammed with callers so the term boiler room, as well as being literal, was a good fit for the high pressure atmosphere in these underground clandestine operations. Picturing a high pressure operation where taxing sales targets are relentlessly pursued conjures up that fierce image of a boiler room. A high octane 'cool room' doesn't create the same cut and thrust image associated with the game.

Quality leads! Quality leads are the lifeblood of the business. Without qualified prospects to pitch the business dies. Fact. I continually experimented with different lead sources in search of a perfect provider. But without doubt, there is no such thing. The very best I could hope for was to buy a pilfered database from another boiler room. I was offered a few over the years and my gang went to town on them. That though, was the icing on the cake. We still needed cake.

Raw data was available in abundance. I could also buy tens of thousands of names and telephone numbers of supposedly known buyers with net worths of this and net worths of that, known buyers of shares, known gamblers, and all sorts of known buyers. But at the end of the day much of this crap was out of date or just completely wrong. The known gambler who'd swear blind he'd never placed a bet in his life, or the known timeshare owner who couldn't stand the thought of owning a timeshare, or perhaps calling someone from a list of so-called medical doctors named Percy only to establish that old Percy, bless his heart, was a ninety year old retired bin man.

As a boss it was crucial I remained mindful of the changing nature of the business. Out in Malaysia back in 2000 I had no idea if there were any other operations like ours in town, or anywhere else for that matter. The attitude back in those days was one of can do regardless of the quality of the leads. It was not unknown to hit data in Eastern Europe and have to make six or seven calls just to find someone who spoke English. But as time goes by things change, and in Barcelona things had changed. It was common knowledge that there were numerous operations in the city and indeed across Spain, some were small set ups with three or fours guys on the phone working from an apartment, all the way up to rooms of thirty, forty or fifty guys all hammering the blower, and it was also common knowledge that by just showing up at any of the city's many Irish bars it would be easy to spot and meet up with pirates from other ships. It's human nature, certainly around the boiler room business, that when things aren't going as planned that the thought of the grass being greener on the other side kicks in. Rarely is it the case, but the last thing a narcissist of a phone pirate wants to hear is that his lack of success lies within. Ultimately I've found that there's no such thing as hard work without results but this concept is lost on individuals that need to be spoon fed. The game could be exciting and the financial rewards huge, but it's a hard game, make no mistake.

The changing nature of the beast meant that to Graham's delight, he was kept busy recruiting. Pirate ships leaked pirates and if I didn't keep on top of this I'd end up with all my dirty rats leaving a sinking ship. One response though, that was guaranteed to get my blood boiling when questioning a guy about his under-performance was "it's the leads", usually delivered in a whining voice. Admittedly, some leads were harder to work than others but if your frame of mind is telling you the leads are shit then that's exactly what they'll be and you won't sell a sausage to a starving man. And I think that's pretty much how things work in all areas of our lives. Frame of mind, belief, positivity and a never say die attitude, all go to creating the perception which in turn manifests the reality. And sometimes the going gets exceptionally tough and sometimes you feel like, what the fuck, when it seems like everything's going against you, but the true honest to goodness phone pirate digs deep and will just keep going, plain and simple, he's after your money and won't stop until he has it. And like I said, this concept can be applied to all areas of our lives. I got knocked back by way more girls than I ever got lucky with, I just realised long ago that the world's beautiful women weren't going to come hunting me down, so what the hell, smile, say hi, something, anything, because once that moment has passed its gone for good. Life is a numbers game for sure, and to put it another way, a closed mouth doesn't get fed.

In view of the fact that the nature of the business was continually changing and that qualified leads were the life blood of the business I was continually thinking outside the box in how to deal with two issues simultaneously. Namely, quality leads and staff retention. Little did I know, but I was about to create a flow in one area that would have me make a complete U-turn in my thoughts regarding the other.

In pursuit of lead nirvana I flew to the Philippines. Manila was fast becoming a call-centre giant on a global scale. Many large international companies basing their customer service, sales and support operations from this vibrant country located in the South China Sea. My plan was to establish a small office of a dozen callers to trawl through raw data to create semi-qualified leads that in turn my fronters back in Spain would turn into fully-qualified leads before handing over to their closer.

The qualification process I intended to implement in Manila was to establish some basic criteria, namely that the phone number was active, the person associated with that number actually was, and if at all possible to establish some level of receptiveness to receiving a follow-up call. I'd do this by having my Filipino callers asking questions such as would the prospect be open to receiving information concerning last minute vacation deals that were sold at only 10% of the original price and property and vehicle auction information not readily accessible normally to the general public, seized property auctions for example that sold houses at ridiculously low prices. I had no idea about these type of opportunities or even if they existed, my sole goal was to get the hook in. I wasn't branching out into these areas but felt I could generate receptive leads based on these types of questions, and my guys in Spain would have a good chance of grabbing their attention with what we were offering, namely Reg S stock and the mouth-wateringly convincing stories we'd fabricate to close the deal.

I also felt that I could set this Asian operation up quickly and at a much lower cost that doing so back in Europe – this was obviously why so many major corporations were moving large chunks of their operations out to the Wild East.

I'd made contact with a real estate agent before leaving Spain, briefing her of my intentions in order I could hit the ground running. In my experience Filipinos are incredibly industrious with a 'can do' attitude which is exactly what I was looking for. Vikki, the real estate agent met me at Ninoy Aquino International Airport and immediately introduced me to her husband, Bong and his Toyota SUV. If I so wished Bong would be my driver and guide for the duration of my stay. Fair enough. Closed. On the drive to one of my favourite hotels in Makati City, The Renaissance, Vikki informed me that she had many contacts and again, if I so wished, she would act as a one-stop-shop for all my requirements, including staff, telecoms, payroll, tax, licenses, legal work and of course the actual office itself . She wasn't a real estate agent, she was a wheeler dealer and a fixer. Just what I needed, and I could only admire her style. I told her 'yes' to all of the above. She turned to me from the front passenger seat, gave a dazzling smile and said "perfect". I love a good closer.

The next week was a blur of activity but I achieved what I'd set out to do. I'd set up my lead qualification room and even struck up a deal with Vikki to manage it. I spent a further three days in Manila once the room went live and was as happy as I could be leaving it in the hands of others once I returned to Spain. I didn't get a huge amount of time to myself so was unable to take a trip out to any of the islands which I'd loved to have done, but I did take all my new guys and gals out for a knees up in Hard Rock Café in the Ayala Centre in Metro Makati. I've visited Hard Rock Cafes around the globe and without a second thought I'd say that the one in Makati is my number one by far. My friend Jaz was singing that night and an incredibly friendly fun night was enjoyed by all. Great country and great people.

Within a month of returning to Barca I discovered something I really didn't expect. I was hoping more than anything else that the room in Philippines would more or less just clean up the raw data I provided for them. It turned out however, that the leads they produced were not just OK, they were good. So good in fact that the closers found they could go into them directly without them having to be re-qualified first by one of their fronting team members. This was a big deal and potentially would change the whole way we did business and the closers would in turn be in a position to make even more money if not having to split commissions with fronters. This changed my view on staff retention completely. I no longer needed fronters in Spain.

Al and I discussed this at length, the end result was that we'd give the current fronters a month to prove themselves as closers or the fat lady would start singing them out of the door.

We ended up with a total of ten competent closers. All now picking up bigger commissions and feeling part of a laser focused, very privileged team. Did someone say staff retention? Two implications became apparent since this turn of events. Firstly, I didn't need three of the company apartments I currently had leased and secondly, our office was too big. But sometimes opportunity presents itself in strange and mysterious ways and when you least expect it.

I was having dinner with Lana in one of my favourite non-sushi establishments, a place called The Speakeasy. The Speakeasy is located in a windowless room at the rear of a fabulous Martini bar aptly named, The Martini Bar. Two dry Martinis in this little haven is enough, I'd discovered, for anyone. Unless, your goal was to get completely shit faced of course. The Speakeasy was representational of a 1920's New York style speakeasy, an illegal drinking hole. To enter this wonderfully secretive gem of a restaurant patrons had to pass through the kitchen, which added to the authenticity of the place by providing a mysterious and genuine speakeasy experience. Private, romantic and with exceptional fare, this was the perfect spot to spend the evening with a beautiful woman. It never got old or less humorous the way the waiter would crinkle his nose at customers menu selections, shaking his head in disapproval, and then indicating what he considered a more suitable choice for a particular guest. Matching dishes to people. Classic. The Brazilian looks out of this world. A woman in her line of work at the level in which she operated knew how to perfect and present her physical being. A smart girl too, with a sharp entrepreneurial spirit.

My entrepreneurial suspicions regarding the lovely Lana were about to be confirmed.

I'd been telling Lana about developments within my business and that I now had some apartments which for want of a better expression, I was stuck with for the foreseeable future. I'd paid some hefty deposits to secure the leases and stood to lose those if I broke the contracts.

Lana had friends in the same line of work and all of them came from countries that would require they had working permits to legitimately work in Spain. Not being official residents meant it was virtually impossible for them to secure apartment leases. Many rented rooms unofficially and plied their trade in some of the city's nicest hotels or at clients houses or apartments. Or boats. Some had 'special' clients that would secure apartments for their girl, but on the understanding that their relationship would be exclusive.

I met several of Lana's friends over the years, all very independent with various financial goals. Usually to make enough money to buy a property back home and set up a legitimate business. Most were in no hurry to be 'kept' in an apartment by some rich dude, unless of course he was prepared to match their income, which on a good months could be in excess of €20,000. Lana was convinced that if any of my apartments were suitable she could rent them out to her friends. The apartment would need to be central, furnished to a high standard and most importantly of all it would need to be without a doorman. Many residential buildings in Barcelona have doormen called porteros who usually live in the building, like a caretaker. El portero, the doorman. Prostitution is not illegal in Spain, but these girls were incredibly discreet, they needed to be as many of their clients were important people, such as high ranking government officials, senior businessmen and even well-known TV personalities.

Lana said she could charge €1500 per month per room, one apartment in particular jumped out as one that may be suitable for what she was proposing. It was a four bedroom, four bathroom attic unit with its own private sun terrace, there was no doorman and it was very central. And ironically enough, was located on a street called Calle Casanova. What the hell, I thought, why not? The apartment was costing me €1500 per month so if Lana could cover that she was welcome to fill her boots. Puss in boots on Calle Casanova.

I dropped by once she'd spruced the place up. She'd spent several thousand euros on doing so and what a huge difference she'd made to the place. From having a bunch of sloppy fronters doing their best to make the place look like a student hovel, it now looked palatial with a subtle and classy sexiness. Soft lighting, huge scented candles, rich colours, plenty of soft furnishings, throw cushions, erotic artwork, chilled music, immaculately clean with a fridge full of beer and champagne. Fair do's, the Brazilian had done a fantastic job.

A year later to celebrate her one year anniversary of moving into Calle Casanova she bought me a 007 edition Omega watch. They say you can't make a housewife out of a whore. Why the fuck would I ever want to? Fabulous girl. Al, not to be outdone by all this apartment fun had decided to pay the rent of one of the other apartments to keep as his love nest. He'd been having a casual-relationship with a Cuban girl since I'd met him and his weekly rendezvous with the dark curly haired Cuban had become somewhat problematic since the Bulgarian Princess had moved in. Always puzzled me that one, but his choice after all. The third of the excess apartments I let go, I lost out on the deposit but sometimes that's just how the cookie crumbles. All that was left now was to figure out what we were going to do about our oversized office. We let that go as well and moved to a more appropriate one on Calle de la Diputacio, a mere stones-throw away from Lana's pleasure palace.

Calle de la Diputacio

The new office in Calle de la Diputacio was at the junction where it crossed with Calle Casanova, centrally located and affluent as most central areas of the city were. As a point of interest, not that it makes any difference to the story, our new office was located smack bang in the middle of the gay district. It wasn't so apparent during daylight hours, although on close inspection there were plenty of tell-tale signs, such as clothes shops with male mannequins holding hands and shamelessly dressed like the Village People as well as a great big whopping rainbow flag hanging outside one of the hotels . As day turned into night however the place became gay-alive with bars and the vast majority of the population on the streets openly gay. It seemed particularly so around the junction on which our new office was located and in fact directly opposite was a gay sauna that I sent Paulo our security guy across to, telling him it was a gym and to enquire about membership. I watched from my office window as he came scurrying back across the street red faced and shook up after realising he'd been set up. He certainly wasn't the sharpest tool in the box.

The move to the new office had gone smoothly. It was perfectly sized for our requirements and we gave the closers new larger desks and executive chairs to create a feeling of privilege and exclusivity in their well-earned positions. The buzz was still there with no real room for an eleventh desk unless we installed smaller ones. It was understood that top performance was expected and there was no room for dead wood, everyone was singing from the same song sheet, we'd created an incredibly efficient machine. Unlike having a bunch of starving fronters roaming around, the closers took things much more seriously and were to a large degree self managing. That said, our most prolific closer, Badger, was somewhat of a nightmare when he'd had a few drinks and always ended up wanting to fight someone, and often did. The sad thing about this recurring scenario though was that he was a completely fucking useless scrapper, and would often enter the office on a Monday morning sporting a black eye or two. A true Jekyll and Hyde character, he gained promotion in the office to manage the other animals under the watchful eye of Paulo, should Al and I be away. In fairness he led well in the office, gave effective and motivational morning meetings and always led from the front. An exceptional closer, which is why it always left me scratching my head when it came to his antics outside the office. One lazy Sunday afternoon as I relaxed on my front terrace surveying the streets below while Natalia sat cross legged on a dining chair beneath the awning editing some photography project on her MacBook Pro, I spotted an unusual scene. From out of nowhere, the tranquil Sunday streets below all of sudden looked like a scene straight out of Braveheart. In Plaza Urquinaona to the right of where I stood I witnessed a bare chested, bare footed, red headed warrior waving what appeared to be a long stick, or possibly a sword, at a group of men who had started to exit and gather outside The George Payne, a popular Irish bar. The lone warrior was shouting abuse and threats at the fifteen or so men who looked none too pleased at this display of bravado. "Hold on" I thought, "no, it can't be" But it bloody was. Badger. I grabbed my pirate telescope (yes, I had a pirate telescope) and zoomed in on the aggressor. Next he launched what I could now see was not a sword but a pool cue at the gathering crowd, scattering them as they moved rapidly to avoid being speared by this high-velocity projectile. The last I saw of badger that afternoon was of him disappearing at a fair lick up a side street as the angry mob charged after him.

Natalia casually looked up from her work asking what I was looking at. "Nothing much" I replied as Isnapped the telescope shut. She already thought I employed a bunch of animals having accompanied me to a get together for something or other only to be subjected to these gentlemen's behaviour in a social setting. I had to admit, we did have our fair share of yobs. Two of the boys, not Badger strangely enough, had been actively involved in the organised football hooligan movement in the UK back in the nineties. Their aggressive alpha male energies now channeled into selling Reg S stock. Being a ruthless thug, but sounding professional and convincing was a distinct advantage it this game.

I'd set up the Manila lead generation office in haste. From arriving in Manila armed with determination and a firm intention, I'd achieved what I set out to achieve in ten days. A few months had past and I owed it to all concerned to head back out to show my appreciation for their hard work and to show that I was interested and involved in what they were achieving. Besides I had ideas about increasing the staff numbers, and a trip out to the islands was definitely a possibility. Al too, was keen to visit the islands after listening to my fun filled stories concerning my previous visits so we decided to make a trip of it together.

Vikki was her usual helpful self and her office was running well. She was making four times as much as she was as a real estate agent so she was certainly committed to the cause. An office twice the size and already call-centre ready had recently become available in the same buildings. We took possession of that and instructed Vikki to max out the room, which would comfortably accommodate twenty five. This pleased Vikki enormously, her earnings would potentially double from an already substantial amount by local standards.

She was on fire. Her handle on everything meant that Al and I were free to have some fun. Our second evening in Makati City was a blur of activity, bars and girls. Back at the Shangri-La, we were camped out in a couple of junior suites, we attempted to go swimming with four local beauties in the very last hour before sunrise but were unfortunately cut off at the pass by security staff, insisting we were in no fit state to go for a dip. The half-drunk bottle of tequila tucked under my arm might have given us away but nevertheless the party continued between our two suites and a damn good time was had by all.

The following evening I hooked up with Jaz, as Al was still recovering from the previous night's shenanigans . Jaz and I had dinner and drinks, and then later still, breakfast. By this time my sparring partner was back from the dead and fighting fit. He joined us, keen to get out to the islands. Jaz suggested we take a boat out to Puerto Galera, it sounded like a great idea so I invited her along. “What about your friend?” She asked in a somewhat concerned manner, not wanting to spoil our boys trip. But Jaz was great to have around and up for most things so I told her it wouldn’t be a problem and he’d enjoy having her around. And anyway, having a local in tow when travelling is always a bonus, a bit like a fixer. Jaz, true to her sporting self, took matters into her own hands after that and decided that my pal Al should have some personal care company of his own in the form of her friend Gemma, who just so happened to be shapely and hot as hell. When she stepped out from the taxi in front of the hotel later that morning we were enjoying a cocktail inside, Jazz pointed out through the floor to ceiling window, “there she is”. Al’s face was a treat. Talk about a Cheshire cat, he was grinning from ear to ear like an complete idiot.

We all spent and idyllic three days on that paradise of an island at a perfect and exclusive beach resort. Al managed to score some nice mellow local weed, which melted away all thoughts and concerns outside our current version of heaven. Aside form the jet skiing and scuba diving in crystal clear waters, my lasting memory is of the bamboo lookout post on the beach. A sort of little hut on long legs with a straw roof and a bamboo ladder to climb up into it. The four of us were up there one evening smoking a bone while admiring a stunning sunset, in fact so awe inspiring that with the girls bent over in front of us, extremely scantily clad, it almost seemed rude not to get a little closer to them, so to speak. It felt a little weird with Al moving back and fore in unison with me and completely put me off my stride when he uttered, “so this is what it feels like to be Tarzan”. I couldn’t go on, so took Jaz back to our luxury beach hut accommodation to continue without the distraction of that wisecracking grizzly bear beside me.

By the time we'd returned to Manila, Vikki had filled all the new caller spots, and with that, increased substantially our daily lead production from our Asian office in the Ortigas business district. Our closers would benefit for sure, thus anchoring their 'loyalty' to our pirate ship further more.

The night before we flew back to Europe we took the entire crew to Hard Rock Café. The jobs we'd created were highly coveted, the guys making less than their European counterparts but still were hitting a home run by local standards. And to be treated to a night out by their British and American bosses was touch they appreciated and I'm sure helped in elevating their already strong work ethic on the phones. Our operation had become a truly global affair. Head office in Barcelona, a lead generation machine in Manila, product from the U.S, banking all over the place and clients everywhere in the English speaking world. It was fair to say that we had it seriously going on.

Back in Barcelona spirits were high with the news of the lead operation developments in South East Asia. Everyone committed to working whatever hours it took to handle the increase most effectively. At a real push I could have crammed another couple of desks in the office if need be and I made the team aware of this, but was assured that wouldn't benecessary, they'd handle the increased workload and sales targets were shifted upwards accordingly. It would have been a completely pointless exercise expanding the Manila operation and not expecting more out of the money end of the machine.

Leads, and business in general, were on my mind when I made myentrance into On Sushi with the delectable Brazilian beauty. We'd turned plenty of heads as we sauntered in, although I suspect most of the neck twisting had been largely due to my companion's presence. As usual she looked elegant and glamorous, even though she was only wearing a tiny white summer dress and tan, heeled sandals. To be fair, she looked good in pretty much anything and tonight was no exception. Absolutely gorgeous. Our conversation flowed as it usually did. Lana's pleasure palace was running as it should, and all was well. Our conversation turned to my recent trip to Asia and my lead operation in that part of the world, when all of sudden it hit me. Hooker leads!

No, I didn't intend to start ramming Reg S stock into the whore community of Barcelona, but perhaps there was potential amongst their clients. After all, these were high class girls charging premium prices, their clients were rich and had the financial ability. They were all obviously thrill seekers after a little of the forbidden fruit, so why not let them take a great big bite out of what I had to offer? My mind started spinning as I thought of the brilliance and audacity of this despicable plan. I mean, a girl would be perfectly placed to reverse engineer these red hot leads from the comfort of her back.

I ordered more saki, it was going down well, and casually mentioned the seeds of my idea to luscious Lana. I didn't need to dress it up at all, she was aware that my business was a little on the shady side, if not completely on the dark side. Lana, as lovely as she was, as beautiful, sweet, as genuine sounding and a sympathetic listener to all, including me, was, when it's all said and done, just the same as me. If she had morals, they must have been somebody else's as they certainly we're hers.

On hearing my idea and the potential for some heavy duty financial gain her entrepreneurial spirit exploded and out popped the devil herself, eyes sparkling and nails glistening. I knew the sex would be out of this world later on that evening, and wasn't wrong.

I hashed out the bones of a plan in which the leads could be generated as I lay there in the early morning light. I drove a very nice car, a sexy car that's associated with wealth and success. Perception is reality, remember. Lana had driven my Porsche on several occasions, so what if Lana was to suggest to a client flying into Barcelona for a couple of days that she pick him up from the airport? A conversation would likely ensue concerning the lovely Lana's awesome piece of German engineering, and the games would begin. Furthermore, what if Lana was to expose the fact that she had bought the car with profits from some of her recent investments? 'Some' of the profits she'd enjoyed from investment ideas and opportunities that had been made available to her by a very special 'friend'. Opportunities so exclusive, so outrageously profitable, that only a select few in the 'know' were ever invited in to benefit from these sure-fire winners.

Let me clarify a couple of things here. Fucking top shelf hookers is a big boy's game. A boys with toys game. It's a pastime that requires a certain amount of discretion (and cash) and a pastime that boosts the boys with toys ego, just as his flashy cars or his amazing houses do wonders for his self-esteem. Yet the high class hooker game, although it's a kind of status symbol, can only be flashed around in restaurants or clubs during clandestine meetings. The arm candy cannot be flashed around in his public life, it's taboo, as well as would obviously cause all sorts of trouble and strife with the wife back at home sweet home.

Investing in high risk stocks over the phone is also, in many clients imaginations, a little like the above mentioned. When presenting our opportunities we would always present them as exclusive in which only a select few were lucky enough to be getting the offer at that particular time. That particular time, being exactly the time we were calling . It was a club, and one in which many clients felt they were getting inside track information. And information not to be shouted from the rooftops, it was for the fortunate, select few. To me, our Reg S opportunities seemed a perfect fit for these big boys with toys. And birds of a feather flock together, so my devilish plan was banking on certain assumptions. Specifically that some ofthese wealthy hooker clients in which my sphere of influence could reach, would actually take the bait and agree to a telephone hook-up with the hooker's hook-up.

All I need do in the first instance was to give Lana the words, and explain the way in which I saw the whole thing unfold and how she should direct operations. In my mind I envisioned a scenario where Lana would absolutely and unequivocally not 'sell' the opportunity or the idea to the client, but to reel him in unwittingly, making him do the chasing and ultimately feel he'd manipulated the information from the girl convincing her to hook him up with her guy. After all, these captains of industry and the like were used to getting their way and controlling others.

My plan was that Al and I would deal with these clients exclusively and not fuck around with small change deals. The only people that would need to be in the know would be me, Al, and the hooker. I figured we'd split this deal three ways equally meaning each of us would end up with twenty five points a-piece. We might even shave a little off each in order to give the client a discount from the market price. A ploy often used. We'd tell clients we'd secured a large block of institutional stock at five points below the market price and were passing this discount on, therefore making the deal seem even more attractive, and putting the client ahead of the game and immediately into a profitable position. Of course the client couldn't sell the shares for a year or more so this 'benefit' actually meant diddly squat.

Lana's juices were certainly flowing once I explained that I saw a million dollar deal, either on its own or collectively from a few of her clients. If this came off she'd pocket two hundred and fifty big 'uns. Nice work if you can get it. She absolutely was one hundred percent up for this and my suspicions were completely confirmed that in conspiring together on a project like this was one hell of an aphrodisiac for the lovely Lana. She wore me out later that night. An enormously enjoyable thrashing to celebrate the hatching of my deliciously despicable plan.

Al, not surprisingly, loved the idea. But my plans to embark later that week on a role playing and complete training package outside the office with the lovely Lana were rudely interrupted when some unwelcome guests came barging in through the doors. It was a film crew from an investigative journalist team, out and about making a documentary about the boiler rooms of Barcelona, their cameras rolling. Unfortunately for them, our guys were no shrinking violets when it came to physical conflict and before they could shout "cut, that's a wrap" were set upon by my enraged pirates, led not surprisingly by one very angry Badger. Seconds later they'd been ejected and were tumbling down the stairs, cameras and sound equipment bouncing around them.

Our location had been compromised to the documentary makers by a disgruntled ex-member of the team who couldn't accept the fact that he wasn't capable of cutting the mustard. Apparently he'd gone to the police first who'd had little interest in his ramblings before hitting on the idea of the TV guys. Their visit left us with little choice, we'd need to seek out alternative accommodation from where to operate. An expensive exercise in both time and money but hey, why take a chance, much better to cut them off at the pass. Our website would need to be reinvented as well which was no great shakes, a quick call to my Croatian web guy and voila, a new website. I'd seen the confusion and shit storm that had been created when J.T and Nad had their banking closed down and I wasn't going to make that mistake. I had several websites ready and waiting in the wings, just as I did bank accounts ready to take over clearing funds should we get the big freeze from whoever we were using at the time.

I thought that we might have lost some guys after the recent intrusion but found them all to be solid and if anything loyalties strengthened. All that is apart from Paulo, our security guy. He talked a good fight but was a bit of a pussy if the truth be known. He was totally aware of the nature of our business and quite happy to benefit financially from our ill-gotten gains but as soon as there was a whiff of trouble in the air from outside he crumbled. He panicked like a frightened child. He cut his hair and shaved his silly little beard off and was never seen again. Never that is, until he was picked up some years later so I believe. Any respect any of the guys had ever had for him plummeted to zero. Franky, I was happy to see the back of the fuckwit.

I didn't want to push our luck after the 'tumbling down the stairs they go' incident so after the guys had made whatever pressing calls they needed to make we locked up and went out drinking. Nothing like a few pirate juices in the face of adversity. Meanwhile our three admin girls got on the case and went to work finding us a new office. With those three tenacious lovelies on a mission I felt we'd have our new home pretty sharpish.

The initial surprise of the unwelcome visit soon wore off and a solution seeking attitude developed all round. Part of our anti-detection strategy from now on would be to do away with our Barcelona P.O Box number and portray ourselves as being located in other locations around the world. Easily done as addresses and telephone numbers for other locations are easily available from numerous sources with answering services and call forwarding standard features. The reason for this was not solely driven by the film crew but because Barcelona was already receiving a lot of media coverage about it as a location for numerous unlicensed brokerage firms such as ours.

Our post invasion drinking session was getting into full swing by late afternoon. Inside on this particular day as it was pissing down outside. When it rains it pours, as they say. The miserable weather didn't reflect the atmosphere inside Café 7 though. Beer and rum were flowing and cocaine seemed to have appeared as if by magic. Our impromptu party was about to get better, for me anyway. Al's Cuban side piece showed up with her friend Shelley. I'd met Shelley once or twice fleetingly and had thought she had 'that look'. The look, that is, of being up for a bit of slap and tickle. Our conversation was extremely candid, Shelley by no means shy in confessing that she was married to an older, rich Austrian dude and their relationship was 'open'. So open in fact that he paid for her to rent an apartment in Barcelona and allowed her to hang out there on her own (well, at least not with him) for two weeks in every month. And according to Shelley, he also gave her €4000 per month pocket money to finance her wild lifestyle. Her words. The straw that broke the camel's back with regards to where this conversation was leading was when Shelley let me know, while pushing her fantastic chest out, that she'd recently had a boob job and after her visit to the doctor earlier this very day had had the all clear and was therefore fully permitted to take them out and have some fun with them. "Perhaps I can take them out for a test drive" I said while fixing her with a laser like stare, though it was hard work not dropping my gaze down to those new DD's. Smiling a wickedly sexy smile Shelley said she needed to go home first but would meet me at my apartment within the hour. Bingo!

I got drenched riding my scooter back to the ranch so jumped straight into the shower, which is where I was when Shelley showed up. Good timing indeed. I wrapped a towel around my waist and headed into the unknown known, to buzz her in.

Shelley entered wearing a raincoat, which was appropriate considering the weather, and looked like a very attractive female version of Colombo, the old-school detective from the TV show. She gave a very naughty smile as she unbuttoned the raincoat having literally just crossed the threshold of my humble abode, opened it wide exposing the delightful sight of her naked body clad only in stockings suspenders and glossy high heels. A spectacular sight to behold.

I perhaps understand why Shelley's husband only wanted her in Austria for half the month. She was insatiable, a rocket and as wild as they come. That day certainly ended way better than it had begun.

The remainder of that eventful week was not surprisingly extremely hectic. The great news though was that the girls had found us a new home. It's easy to say, I know, but the office we were now heading to was even more perfect that the one we'd just been busted at on Calle de la Diputacio. Calle d'Enrique Granados had always been one of my favourite streets in Barcelona and our new office was located on the junction of Calle d'Enrique Granados and Caller del Rossello, an area in which some of my favourite bars and restaurants were located. On Sushi, Non Solo Pizza and The Martini Bar were virtually on our doorstep, not to mention an English style pub and a superb kebab house. I have no idea whether we had any more unwanted visitors in the Calle de la Diputacio office as within a week of the showdown there was no sign we'd ever been there. It had been a tough week with all hands on deck shifting and humping our gear out of Dodge, but it was done, and by the start of the following week it was business as usual. The phones and our clients taking a hammering once again. The whole thing had been nothing more than a hiccup in the scheme of things. And our pirates showed their true pirate colours in embracing the challenge and driving on through.

The downtime between X and Y was spent productively in a slightly different kind of way for one of our guys. Pete had a guy on the ropes who'd openly boasted that he illegally dealt in recreational drugs, and consequently had cash that he wanted to use to fund a small investment. If we could accommodate a Western Union transfer he was in. Trouble was, he was under the impression we were located in Switzerland, so it stood to reason that that's where he'd expect to transfer his cash. As Pete had time on his hands he thought what the hell, finalised the details with his client, jumped on an EasyJet and popped over to Zurich to pick up around €12,000.

Later that evening Pete showed up at my place with the cash. A true Phone Pirate. I counted out his share and added a bonus before calling Lana and telling her to pick out one of her friends for Pete, as I'd be bringing him over after we'd had a puff and a couple of pirate juices. All, of course, courtesy of the firm. After dropping a smiley faced Pete off at the pleasure palace Lana and I headed for Non Solo Pizza. Miss Brazil was eager to tell me about a German businessman that was flying in for a weekend convention the week after next. She'd already suggested she collect him from the airport on this occasion to which, according to Lana, he seemed agreeable. My initial thought as I imagined the Brazilian tooling around Barca in my Porsche was that perhaps I'd been a little rash in offering up my ride as a prop in this crazy project. Though I quickly checked and corrected my thinking. I was in the business of bringing outlandish and unreasonable ideas to fruition. Besides, if I reneged now on what had been my idea in the first place I'd look like a complete pussy in front of this ravishingly beautiful woman, who, was quite clearly up for the challenge. So basically, it was game on. It was also quite an amusing thought that if anything came of this, between Shelley's hubby and

Lana's 'friend' the old Krauts would be taking a right old shafting. By now, I was getting used to Lana's increased sex drive at the thought of us delivering on this scheme, so in actual fact, the only good old shafting that took place on this evening was back where I hung my hat.

I'm perfectly aware that my behaviour at this time in my life was off the charts. Instead of thinking that it was perhaps time to throw in the towel after the investigative documentary team burst in to our lives, it was like a red rag to a bull inasmuch as I had no intention of stopping, and stand in my way at your peril. If the truth be known I was also relishing our notoriety amongst other rooms in the city. We had to be doing something 'right' if the bastards wanted to make a TV documentary about us. On the day of the raid, instead of inward reflection, I took my guys on a drug and alcohol fueled bender where they swore allegiance to the cause, and that saw me ending my night hanging out of the back of a Austrian businessman's Cuban wife, while juggling her brand new fun bags. Days later I was conspiring with a Brazilian prostitute in order to extract as much money as possible from one of her Johns while we fine dined for the first part of the evening then bounced around my apartment like a couple of porn stars for the remainder. In my world, clients were faceless, merely voices on the end of the phone. They weren't real people with real lives, aspirations and families. And even if I'd tried to I couldn't have conjured up images of our clients lives. They meant nothing to me other than a means to personal gain. I was driven completely and utterly by thoughtless greed. To put it another way, I just didn't give a fuck. In fact our clients were a necessary nuisance. It would have been far easier if they'd just send us all their money in the first place saving us the pointless task of buying bullshit stock on their behalf and running an office full of lunatics. It would have freed me up to concentrate on my own selfish ends of fast women, fast cars and fast living. A completely unsubstantial waste of life.

But I wasn't about to stop anytime soon, I was completely blinded by the light, or more to the point, completely consumed by darkness. Hurricane Me had not yet reached the Eye Wall of its destructive power, and as I sat looking out onto my newest sales floor, I glanced at my 007 edition Omega watch that Lana, the whore with the cover girl looks, had given for me, and I thought, I'm the fucking Bond Villain. And I smiled at the thought. I was out of control and I'd completely lost the plot.

Calle d'Enrique Granados

"It's not important that you don't know what inside information means" I said to the Brazilian beauty as we lay in bed the Friday morning of the day she was planning to collect Fritz from El Prat International airport in my gleaming Black Porsche. And, it wasn't important that she didn't really understand it. In fact the less she understood about the mechanisms of the supposed investments I'd supposedly been feeding her the better. Lana was a great conversationalist, able to steer a conversation as well as the best sales guys out there, and she completely understood that she and Fritz had to arrive at a stage in their little chess match where our German friend felt he had cornered Lana into revealing the information and thus check mating her. Fritz had to feel in charge, he needed to believe he was in control, that he'd got what he wanted and not in the slightest feel the control was with our girl. Lana understood perfectly well either by instinct or intention how to close, was a great actress, knew how to make a man feel good in any social situation, and not surprisingly, knew exactly how to float a guy's boat in the sack. I was incredibly curious to see how her skills were put into practice, and would have loved a ring-side seat for the up and coming event. Unfortunately though, I'd have to rely on Miss Brazil's recounting of events in due course. Having said that, Lana did know how to spin a pretty good yarn and I was looking forward to the next time we'd meet to hear the blow by blow account of how things panned out.

After a full English cooked by yours truly, Lana sashayed off armed with my car keys and her bad intentions, while I hopped on my trusty steed and scootered to the office.

Friday was an especially feel good day with us usually knocking off around 4pm provided we'd achieved our weekly targets. Café 7 religiously the beneficiary of our company and our drinking cash. Al and I didn't discuss Lana although he was aware she was on a mission. I could tell he wasn't particularly optimistic that anything would come of it and he'd even aired his opinion that I was crazy to let a hooker disappear into the sunset with my sixty thousand euro motor. Maybe I was, but we weren't exactly in the non-risk taking business, and perhaps our antics of bouncing around the city from one office to another, like a pinball, might not be looked on as the sanest behaviour in the world either. Anyway, I was enjoying the thrill and the nervous energy was giving me a buzz. I glanced at my watch as Al ordered more beer for everyone, and smiled, knowing that Lana that fantastic specimen, would be at this very moment turning heads in traffic as she gunned my 911 through the beautiful streets of Barcelona en route to her rendezvous with Herr Fritz.

Now I know this sounds flippant, and she hasn't made an appearance in this story as yet and is unlikely to again, but I was also seeing another Brazilian, Gina. We'd go months without seeing each other, then out of the blue, this single mum would call me. Or vice versa. If neither of us had anything else on we'd usually hook up. I'd bung a oner at her overnight baby sitter and we'd generally party 'til dawn. Usually this translated to dinner and a coke fuelled night back at my place. Gina was physically very beautiful, but also as nutty as a fruit bat. Any prolonged or more frequent relationship between us would have turned toxic. When I say Gina was beautiful I don't throw the term around easily. She was thirty years old and to me didn't look any different than she did in the Brazilian edition of Penthouse that she'd featured in seven years earlier as 'Pet of the Month'. Not traditionally Brazilian looking, her grandparents were Polish on her mother's side and her father

Fully northern European as well. The combination had left her with fair skin, a fine bone structure and piercingly green eyes. She didn't push me for any more than we had and I think she was probably happy just to use me as an outlet from single parenthood. I was happy enough to oblige. I called Gina from Café 7 and within a few hours we were sat in her favourite Chinese restaurant. The evening progressed as expected but did little to distract me from wondering how it was going at Hotel Arts where Lana was on the job. Don't get me wrong, I had a good time and actually saw Gina on and off for a good two years, but apart from the predictable nature of our meetings there's not much else to say. She was a great piece of ass and we both served a purpose for the other. A cold interpretation but an accurate one nonetheless. Gina left contented Saturday morning leaving me to rattle around my apartment waiting for Lana to report in. Talk about restless, I was on pins. I hit the gym to try to release some of my pent up energy and let the sauna do its job in helping me sweat out the excesses of the previous night. I scooted home, rolled a bone and settled down in front of Sky Sports to wait. Five o'clock came and went and the Brazilian hooker still hadn't reported in and my mind started to wander. Had Al been right about me handing her my keys? My 911 could now be literally anywhere in Europe, Africa even. "That fucking bitch" I thought "I knew I shouldn't have trusted that smiling assassin who was no better than.." and then my phone rang. Miss Brazil. She was her normal cheery self and wanted to know if I fancied dinner later, and suggested she pick me up at around nine. Cheeky tart.

In reality I was happy enough but would be lying if I said I didn't feel some sense of relief that she hadn't 'done one' with my wheels. I told her to keep enjoying the car and that I'd see her later as she suggested. Hopefully it had all been worth it and our boy Fritz had taken the bait.

She called ten minutes before arriving to let me know she'd be outside, as there was no parking directly outside my gaff, and even doing so for ten minutes would draw the traffic police like bees to honey. I was down stairs in five. It gave me a charge watching her pull up looking like a movie star and totally at home in the Batmobile. I hopped in, she put her foot down, and off we roared. "Speakeasy OK?" She said, "my treat". She glanced across at me with a conspiratorial wink. I was in my element, life was damn good.

Lana had had the foresight to book a table at The Speakeasy much earlier the previous day. Wandering in on a Saturday night and expecting to be seated was just not going to happen. Sat in this superb little restaurant with its rich and warm atmosphere, its subtle lighting, magnificent service and splendid food, I felt as close to the Brazilian hooker as I'd felt to anyone ever. It was a fleeting feeling but a real one all the same. Lana had obviously had some sort of result with Fritz as she'd looked like the cat that had got the cream, completely pleased with herself ever since I'd hopped into my ride, but had been told "wait" when I'd asked "well?". Now, in this wonderful environment it was time to spill the beans. Her eyes smiled and sparkled as she gave me a knowing smile. Fingers interlocked she rested her perfect chin on the backs of her hands and leaned slightly forward. "Where shall I start?" She said. Holy crap, this was turning me on already. "Right from the very start, I want to know every single fucking detail" I told her. Raising an eyebrow she very seductively answered me. "Every detail?" she said, way too sexily. I swear, I was already getting hard.

Now, I can only tell you what Lana told me. I have no way of knowing if it actually happened like this at all. All I can say is that she was completely believable and I had no reason to believe it didn't happen exactly as she described.

Fritz is not this German guy's name, but a name I introduced into proceedings early on and accepted by our girl. He was by all accounts a good looking but slightly strange fellow who, whenever visiting Barcelona would meet up with the classy looking brunette in a Groundhog Day version of their last meeting. His fantasy seemed to play out in exactly the same way each time. Usually he'd meet her in the lobby of the hotel. He would require her to arrive and ask for him at reception. She'd inform the reception staff that Erica from Munich Business Solutions or some other made up firm, had arrived. She'd be wearing the classic secretary get-up; high patent leather heels, black sheer stockings with the line running up the back, black pencil skirt and a tight white cotton blouse. She'd be wearing a pair of black horn rimmed glasses and her hair would be up in a French twist. She'd also be carrying a sleek black Mont Blanc leather business case complete with shoulder strap which contained a Mont Blanc organiser and fountain pen. Fritz would arrive from his room some ten minutes later and they'd sit in the lounge bar in a formal manner making polite small talk, which to any casual observer would look as Fritz intended – a businessman in a business meeting with a beautiful business woman or perhaps his secretary. After a short while Fritz would ask Lana/Erica to take some notes at which point she'd remove the organiser and pen and start scribbling away as Fritz dictated various gobbledygook. Although a handsome and virile looking man, immaculately turned out, Lana would get frustrated by this predictive routine, each visit virtually a carbon copy of the last. Fritz obviously got a kick from the role play, and why not, it was his money, right? The problem was that Lana was a vivacious woman who was incredibly spontaneous, loved to laugh and loved to get well and truly...well, let's just say, loved sex.

This last point created additional frustrations for our girl, because as well as being a little on the rigid and predictable side in their pretend business meetings, he was also extremely predictable in the bedroom. Fritz had some unique ideas about fidelity. Married, he didn't consider the contact between he and Lana in the bedroom constituted cheating. Frau Fritz may have disagreed, but we'll never know.

The evening would progress from the hotel lounge to the Michelin Star restaurant located within the hotel, before the boss and his secretary would retire to his suite for the night. Back in the room a bottle of Champaign would be popped before Fritz would slowly remove his clothes before carefully hanging them in the wardrobe. Apparently he even folded his socks and boxers and slipped them into a drawer while Lana, still fully dressed, waited patiently. Next Fritz would move to the bed and lie on his back while Lana removed her shoes while remaining straight faced while still waiting expectantly. With no further ado Fritz would shout "mouth" at which point Lana, still fully clad apart from the missing shoes, glasses still atop her schnozzle and hair still French twisted, would crawl slowly up the bed and start working him with her mouth. Fritz would be yakking away in Kraut while at the same time according to Lana, thrusting his generous German sausage deep into the Brazilian's oral orifice. I must admit it was an incredible turn on listening to this exceptionally beautiful woman recount her experience in such a detailed and erotic manner. She knew exactly what she was doing. Although, I did start to find the next part more amusing that erotic, in fact it was all I could do to not burst out laughing. Lana continued that next he'd shout "feet" at which point Lana would come up for air, hitch up her tight skirt, sit back, her hands supporting her weight on the bed behind her and then start work his bulging bratwurst with her stockinged feet. This would continue for a while before Fritz would cease from his ramblings and shout "breasts". Our girl would then kneel between his thighs and unbutton her blouse, unclip the front fastening black bra and proceed to continue the merry-go-round using her wonderful Brazilian tits. This would continue for some time, Fritz shouting "feet" or "mouth" or "breasts" with Lana responding accordingly, until eventually, no longer able to contain himself Fritz would release the mother-load, usually on the breast cycle according to our girl. As no penetration of Lana's lady box had taken place Fritz did not consider that in any way shape or form that he'd cheated on Mrs. Fritz. The lovely Lana however, would come away from the experience feeling unsatisfied. She didn't even stay the night, leaving in jeans, t-shirt and sneakers that she'd brought in a Hugo Boss overnight shoulder bag. She'd shower first obviously as by the sounds of things Fritz could have been in the German Olympic nut-blasting team – Captain perhaps. Lana had a healthy sexual appetite if she found a man attractive, and although Fritz was a bit of a bore, Lana did fancy him physically and said, and I quote, "had a beautiful big one".

By this stage my heart was beating like a drum and all I wanted to do was get home and play mouth, feet, tits with the South American sex-bomb, but her story was only just beginning. What she'd told me about so far was what 'usually' happened and she'd yet to tell me what actually had happened on this most recent little get together with the Fritzter. I had the brief thought of what the hell had she been doing with my motor all this time if once he'd hosed her down he basically kicked her out, but quickly dismissed the idea, this was just too good to be interrupted, and quite frankly I didn't give a shit. "So go on then" I said, encouraging her to keep spilling the beans.

Lana could tell immediately as she pulled up outside arrivals and saw Fritz standing there that he was impressed, his 'secretary' pulling up in a 911 looking like the hottest secretary on the planet. "Oh come on Fritz, I only meet a select few friends" Lana had replied when Fritz commented that business must be good as they pulled away from international arrivals. It seems his inquisitiveness got the better of him, as was the plan, and it wasn't too long before Fritz was to ask, whose was the car? Not even fifteen minutes into the journey and only half way to Hotel Arts and our boy was taking the bait. "So if you don't mind me asking.." he continued, it seemed Fritz wanted to know a whole lot more. Lana went on to explain that she felt the dynamic had changed even at this early stage in their exchange, it was as if the shoe was on the other foot, and now Fritz wanted something other than what he'd already paid for. He wanted information. "I invest a little" Lana replied flashing him a brilliant smile. I couldn't help smiling too at this clever, confident girl. " Not large amounts though, but this car is a gift to myself for a good six months". Fritz's brow furrowed, "and how much is not much?" He had smelling blood it seemed and wanted yet more information. "I'm just a poor working girl" continued Lana with a coy pout of her perfect lips, " so not much". Lana could tell this answer was not satisfactory for the German who was a stickler for the details it seemed in all areas of his life, "yes, but how much" he almost barked his reply, then cleared his throat before apologising for his mini outburst. "Well like I said" said Lana "not much, I started six months ago with fifty thousand"

“Euros?”

“Dollars”

“Hmm”. Fritz’s wheels were turning, Lana could almost hear them grinding away in his head. “So you bought this car with your actual profits?”

“Some of them, Yes”

“Some of them?”

“Yes, some of them”. And so it went on. Lana had me captivated, but it was only about to get better. Fritz was eager to know more but they were now drawing close to the hotel. Lana had thought this through and didn’t want to get away from the usual structure of their meeting, if she entered the hotel with him now he may lose his focus, perhaps feel uncomfortable or distracted. Much better to let him enter alone, freshen up and stew in his own thoughts of what the hell Lana was investing in that enabled her to enjoy what appeared to be some absolutely phenomenal returns. She would meet him later as per usual and continue her Trojan horse attack from there. Lana was more than literally in the driver's seat by this stage. Fritz seemed a little disappointed that Lana had made her excuses to leave just as his juices were starting to flow, but accepted her departure gracefully. No doubt he knew he could continue his inquisition once he had Lana where he wanted her, as his parting shot was, "I look forward to hearing more about your investment strategy"

"OK big boy" Lana flirtatiously replied before hitting the gas. Part one of the plan seemed to have been a resounding success.

Our main course arrived and I told Lana to relax. We discussed elements of what had happened up to this point but I felt that the next part of the story would be better explained by

Miss Brazil once we'd polished off this fine cuisine. We did, and she continued.

Hotel Arts at 9pm, Lana and Fritz met in the lounge bar just past the reception area, and in my mind's eye I saw the sultry secretary sashay in like a catwalk model. After drinks were ordered, and small talk dispatched, Fritz delivered his opening gambit, "so, these investments" he said sitting back in his chair expectantly, arms folded. Lana felt confident enough to remove the Mont Blanc organiser and fountain pen from their case and hand them to Fritz, "tonight, you will take the notes if you're so interested" she said, flashing him her most flirtatious smile. A man melting look if ever there was one. Fritz smiled and seemed happy to play along, leaned forward and took the bait. Perhaps this role reversal was giving our boy a thrill. Lana explained to Fritz that she considered him a special friend and one of only several that she could count on the fingers of one hand. It was one of these very special friends who'd grown to trust Lana, and in turn had introduced her to some extremely privileged information, and a straightforward route to capitalising on said information. These were, as Lana's 'friend' had explained to her, 'very privileged and discreet situations'. Fritz was scribbling away furiously, quite obviously under the ether. "What exactly do you mean by privileged and discreet situations?" Lana was vague but ultimately did mention something about inside information. At this the already perky Kraut perked up even more. "Inside information" he whispered excitedly. "Fritz, please, I told you I don't know specifics and I think this conversation has already gone on too long, and I think I've already probably said too much". But Fritz wasn't going to be blown off so easily, "come on Erica", he still called our girl by her whore handle, "you can trust me", and was as close to pleading as Lana had ever seen this man. Lana responded accordingly, “look Fritz, all I know is that three times in the last six months my friend has called me and told me that something is about to make money and if I want to wire funds to some bank or clearing agent or something, so I can get involved” She sighed, “he’ll send me he instructions”, acting as if she were tired of the turn their conversation had taken, and that Fritz was overstepping the mark. It was around ten by now and they were invited to take their seats for dinner. Without going into the specifics of what they ate, drank and talked about outside of our little plan I can tell you that at some time during dinner Fritz asked Lana for the hook up with her special friend. Lana was silent for a moment, stared down at the tablecloth and gathered her composure. She looked up and looked directly into the German’s eyes, “well” she said “I have introduced one other very special friend already so I suppose it’s possible, but” and she paused, “but what Erica?” Said our eager beaver, now looking visibly flustered by all accounts. “Well, I’m enjoying being the one holding all the cards this evening” she said with a naughty smile while maintaining eye contact with the big German fish. Fritz regained his composure at this stage and sensed Lana wanted something from him for this information. Now he felt back in control. If this girl wanted to score a couple of grand for the hook up then no biggie, she was after all just a whore. “Let me ask you a question Erica?” He said, now full of confidence and in somewhat of a smug manner, “what is your real name?”. Without missing a beat our girl replied. “Lana” she said. “ And what exactly is it you want, Lana” said Fritz, leaning back in his chair and folding his arms once again. He was now fully expecting the justification spiel from Lana in her request for a few grand as an introduction fee, and who could blame him. Instead, Lana leaned forward, put one delicate elbow on the table, rested her chin on the back of her hand and looked directly into the German's, "you. Inside me", she said. Fucking classic! Fritz wasn't expecting that one for sure, as he reacted by sitting bolt upright in his chair, "I thought maybe you'd want an introduction fee or something Lana" he blurted out. "Please Fritz, we're friends, right?" She said, leaning back in her chair, once again fully in control, and asked, "So what's it going to be".

It seems Lana got exactly what she wanted, although I felt it was a little too much information when she said it was probably the best session she'd ever had. I may have even pouted a little until she corrected herself by saying 'working session' which had the effect of delivering a great big grin to my face, and my ego too.

What a lead. Talk about red hot. Fritz was absolutely gagging for it. So much so he'd broken his own infidelity rules and banged the Brazilian. Sex that night with Lana was on an intergalactic scale, and we didn't even play paper, scissor, stone. After all was said and done, Lana had done a superb job in creating what can only be described as a million dollar lead. She'd done her part, the rest was down to me. Shooting from the hip had been a life-long speciality, I was ready, and as soon as the weekend was done, I was going in.

I had a telephone in my apartment that was connected to the office system. In fact I could unplug it and plug it in anywhere in the world and as long as I had a WIFI connection I could dial a few digits to connect to any extension in the office. As my hooker lead was on a need to know basis I decided to do the necessary from my gaff. When I'd parted company with the Brazilian late Sunday morning, I let her know I'd be doing just that the following day. Her excitement was palpable even though I explained that nothing might come of it, and I never started counting the money until it was in the bank. What a prospect said he was going to do and what he actually did didn't always equate to the same thing once he'd put the phone down and the cold reality of what he'd just agreed to sunk in. Buyers' remorse can hit even when you think the deal is airtight. She said that yes she understood, but I certainly couldn't see any damping down of her excitement levels.

D-day came and I made a leisurely breakfast after spending an hour at the gym, something I always did provided the pirate juice flu didn't keep me away. An hour well spent charging up for the day ahead. I planned to call Fritz somewhere between ten and eleven and while preparing my second espresso the Brazilian called. "Morning handsome, need a secretary today?" Phone pirates are performers, and as I liked to remind the guys, the only difference between us and actors is that actors still got paid for a bad performance. So yeah, why not? She could come over. I had no idea as to her motives. Perhaps she wanted to make sure I gave my best performance because she was watching, or perhaps she would just get a kick out of watching me on the phone talking to a guy she'd set up for this whole sting. More than likely, I decided it was probably just ants in her pants making her want to know the outcome as soon as possible. Getting the results live so to speak. Well, if she was coming over I might as well have a bit of fun at the same time I thought, "you start work in an hour. Dress appropriately", I said.

I knocked back my second espresso and jumped in the shower. I felt calm and focused, I knew my target, and I knew the stance I'd take. I knew I was good at this, and very convincing. I dressed for success because that's what I always did. It wouldn't have been the same pitching in my underpants. A black Boss suit and grey shirt seemed to fit the bill. I slipped on my 007 watch as a lucky talisman and because this was Lana's deal, just as my 'secretary' buzzed to come in. "Are those real glasses" were my fist words to the one hell of a fit looking secretary look-a-like that had just entered my domain. "No, just normal glass" she said matter-of-factly, as she clip clopped across my solid oak wooden floors. "Sit down. Don't talk" I instructed as I pointed at my four thousand euro Italian leather sofa. I hooked on my earpiece, took a couple of slugs of mineral water and made the call. Fritz answered his mobile on the second ring. "Hello Fritz, this is John. We have a mutual friend, I believe you're expecting my call". I announced confidently from the centre of my room, arms folded and looking down at our mutual friend sat expectantly on the sofa. Fritz sounded serious and business like, just as I'd expected from the vision I'd conjured up of him during Lana's story telling. We didn't discuss our mutual friend beyond my initial introduction. I did not introduce any organisation I represented but rather went on to explain that I was something of an anomaly inasmuch that it would be difficult to categorise the service I provided for my clients, suffice to say that my tentacles of influence and access to information reached far and wide and the inside track information I had an uncanny knack of unearthing meant that my clients were happy to pay a premium for that information that was quite clearly worth its weight in gold, as well as the route to purchase I provided as part and parcel of the whole deal. Additionally, I explained, I was sometimes able to access institutional type trades, never before open to private investors, and facilitate those trades at a five point discount against the market price. I could tell Fritz was buying this crap even though his responses were little more that grunts along the way. "For my information and route to purchase Fritz, I charge five percent of your speculation" I got a couple of positive sounding grunts. Good stuff, he was still with me and I'd got an affirmative on a pre-closing question. I winked at Lana who was looking increasingly delicious as I continued my march towards Fritz's stash. I had no intention of opening Fritz with a shitty five or ten grand trade. This was totally different than the normal way of building a client, this was a hooker lead and was going to go down in a completely different way. It'd be all or nothing. Fritz was a different kettle of fish. He'd seen the spoils of Lana's speculation, shit he'd been driven round in the spoils, and heard directly from her delicious lips that I was the guy to do business with, if I decided I'd do business with you. I went on to explain to Fritz that when I brought him an idea I didn't want to tap dance around selling him on it, that's not how I operated or how this thing worked. My clients understood that I wasn't necessarily at liberty to discuss how I came by my information and why I was so convinced of my recommendations. "When I come to you Fritz the only thing I'm interested in is how much you're good for". I could tell by Fritz's increased uh-huhs that I was doing a good job and he was being led to the sacrificial alter without me having to backtrack at all. I suppose my initial pitch lasted seven or eight minutes but seemed much quicker as I was enjoying myself. I especially enjoyed his questions when I got to the end of my spiel and asked him, "so Fritz, questions?". "How do I purchase?" and "do you have anything in the pipeline?" I think were my favourite two but all were sending huge buying signals. I especially enjoyed his last question as to whether I had anything in the pipeline. "Well it just so happens Fritz" I began as I walked over to where Lana was sitting and stood directly in front of her as she perched on the edge of my sofa looking rather flushed. I could almost hear her heart beating. She did look great as a sexy secretary, peering up at me over the top of her black rimmed 'just glass' glasses. "Timing is everything, and timing couldn't be better for us today". And off to the races we went.

As I was closing up the call with Fritz I mouthed the word 'mouth' to my lovely secretary, who, like the excellent secretary she was, expertly undid my belt and Hugo Boss strides. I was still saying ' welcome on board and we'll speak soon' when Lana started her oral dictation.

Fritz had agreed to an opening trade of five hundred thousand dollars and my little whore had just made a hundred and twenty five grand. The session that followed was a corker!

Hooker leads, who would have thought? Fritz was the first of a few to bear fruit, but with Fritz it had been a perfect storm, everything just slotted into place. And although between us, Lana and I raised close to three million dollars in the months that followed, there were plenty of occasions when we got blown out, plain and simple. I'd wait for Lana to report in only to hear her tell me that the guy hadn't bitten. We discussed bringing other girls in but for one reason or another in all but one case it never worked out. Lana was one in a million and it seemed it could only work with her. Most other girls didn't grasp what we were doing or understand how to play it, or their grasp of the English language was not sufficient enough to create the intrigue to reel the guy in. That said, Lana did bring one reasonably competent girl into the fray. A Ukrainian girl, Daria. I'm not complaining in the slightest, it was a blast, the whole thing was just such incredible fun, I'm just pointing out that not every 'friend' of the girls dropped their draws, and those that did didn't always chuck in six figures, they didn't all pack the great big balls that our good friend Fritz did. Developing this side of the business also kept me out of the office which I grew to like more and more. Imagine that, preferring the company of fantastically beautiful women over a bunch of testosterone filled Neanderthals.

Time passes and things change. People change. Ambitions change and business partnerships develop or diminish. Al's and mine was about to develop. We were killing it, Al overseeing the office, and while I was still a regular presence in the office, I spent more and more time away developing our very unconventional, yet profitable lead source. Not surprisingly it was the most fun I'd ever had selling Reg S stock. But it wasn't all without it's stories of disaster. On one occasion Lana was entertaining a young privileged fuckwit who'd gotten so drunk he threw up in my car on the way back to the hotel. Daddy paid for everything and this moron had no interest in investing and daddy had no interest in listening to anyone who'd come to him through associations with his idiot of a son. My car stunk of puke for ages, and even after having it valeted twice I still imagined I could smell it.

Success however, far outweighed those mini-disasters, Al and I were building up a nice bit of wedge, even at the rate we'd spend it. And we both had the same feelings regarding branching out, and both fancied the idea of our own bar or restaurant. We explored the possibilities and our exploration led to a decision to make it a reality. We spent a lot of times in restaurants and bars looking at them in a completely different light. A couple of months after we'd started our search we purchased a traspaso (a business lease) on an existing restaurant in the El Borne district of the city. It had been operating as a Moroccan restaurant which is not something either of wanted to continue. Our idea was not to take over a going concern but to create something from scratch, something slick, five star and first class. In other words we wanted it to be the dogs bollocks. We hired a top Argentinian designer who'd designed some of the top bars and clubs in Ibiza as well as having a hand in some major projects in Barcelona. We completely gutted the place. Materials, furniture, fittings and all sorts of crap were imported from Italy and elsewhere, and a crew of guys worked endlessly it seemed. Yet Spain has a slightly different work ethic than say, the Philippines, and progress was slow. Slow or not, progress was made and it gradually started to take shape.

We'd commissioned one of the city's top P.R companies to promote the bar prior to opening night with editorials appearing in all of Spain's top lifestyle papers and magazines. We'd secured a top head chef, and a Spanish manager who'd previously run a fabulous restaurant in one of the city's best nightclubs. Natalia was our photographer and hired a premier web design company.

We installed the latest payment and security systems, state of the art audio visual equipment for the small club and cocktail bar on the lower level, and we hired beautiful staff, top notch chefs, and we'd ultimately hire some of the best up and coming DJ's around. The work and detail that went into our creation was immense with no expense being spared.

Eventually opening night arrived. It had cost the best part of a million euros to bring about this day, a large proportion of that being funded through hooker leads. Hey, somebody had to pay and it sure as hell wasn't going to be us.

Opening night was out of this world. The first of many filled with weird and wonderful happenings in our New York style sushi, cocktail bar and club, Lower East Side, or L.E.S.

Lower East Side Sushi & Drinks

Lower East Side Sushi &Drinks, or L.E.S as it came to be known, just like every other aspect of my lifestyle had been funded by completely ill-gotten gains. The place was exceptional, and one hell of a prop for my philandering ways. Ultimately though, it would ensure the end of mine and Al's business partnership and friendship. Our time together had been one heck of a fast and furious ride, but like everything else, either good or bad, it had to come to an end.

I guess about a year before we opened L.E.S I'd patched things up with my original business partner in the Rambla Catalunya office, Jeff. Jeff had sorted himself out and was running a small operation with a Londoner called Trevor. I'd been over the moon to see Jeff and his girlfriend Lou attend the opening night and have such a good time. All my pirates attended too and paid especially close attention to the open bar. Thankfully most of them were snorting coke so they didn't have a great appetite for the food we had on offer. It would have been devoured in seconds if not for the Colombian marching powder. Our gay manager Frankie was really very well connected with much of the city's 'in' crowd and there were plenty of beautiful people on show that first night. Plenty of Frankie's gay friends too, which I thought was fantastic. Gay men seemed to spend more money on the finer things in life and equally as importantly where I was concerned, always seemed to attract beautiful women in their wake. Early on it became quite apparent that Al didn't like the rainbow people enjoying L.E.S, which, for the reasons I've mentioned above, I just couldn't understand. Natalia accompanied me on opening night and mentioned that she'd had a conversation with Al who had made it perfectly clear what he thought about all the gays prancing around. My thoughts were exactly the opposite, I thought they brought a vibrancy and a sort of approval to the joint. If the most 'in' gays in the city liked L.E.S my thoughts were that we'd do well. The idea was to make money after all. These early rumblings from Al however told me that he wanted to force a certain clientele into the place rather than let it develop organically. My thoughts from the outset were to yes, be around a fair bit but to let Frankie get on with the day to day operations, I wanted him to have free reign to do what he did best. Al on the other hand wanted to be hands-on and to my mind this was a big mistake. We made our money on the phone, lots of it, and I didn't like the idea of my business partner farting around arranging flower deliveries and the like. It was completely unnecessary and a huge waste of his time The Reg S game was getting much harder with documentaries and media coverage that kept going on about the dangers of investing over the phone after being cold called. They were springing up all over the shop, and more and more potential investors were shying away. That didn't mean the business was dead, far from it, it just meant we couldn't afford to be fucking around checking on stupid shit in L.E.S. We needed to keep our focus on where the real money was. Al's focus however, was firmly fixed on the restaurant, he also wangled it so that the lovely Penka, his live in girlfriend, started working alongside Frankie. She had managed a small bar previously and I had no doubt in her ability, but couldn't help thinking that this wasn't a great idea. She'd work in the office for a few hours in the morning attending to matters for both businesses then head down to the restaurant in the late afternoon. She was a very capable and organised woman so I didn't really have any grounds to object. And I suppose it wasn't necessarily a bad decision, though it only strengthened Al's resolve to take over the running of the place completely. Or to get well and truly in the way of its success depending on your school of thought. As I had anticipated, a clash between Al and Frankie was imminent, and I soon got a call from Al as he was out buying fresh flowers forthe restaurant tables, "I've fired the faggot fuck". Yes, as he was out buying flowers. I can't say I was over the moon. We continued to have our fair share of gay customers but not nearly as many as we'd had when Frankie had control. He knew hundreds of social super-stars. Al knew diddly squat. What the hell was he thinking?

"So what's the plan Stan?" I eventually asked him knowing full well what his answer would be. "Me and Penka will run it" came the thoroughly expected reply. We'd both individually taken the initiative on things in the past – me and my hooker leads for example – and it had always worked out, so I didn't feel I had a good enough argument against this latest news. I thought long and hard about it and could see both pro's and con's to the new arrangement. Plus we'd spent a shed load of money on the place too. I let it roll, though I couldn't help feeling the office would suffer. Al had been very hands-on while I'd been out developing the hooker leads, an area that was still profitable, so I was concerned but kept much to myself. I was already hearing that little voice in my head, why take a chance, cut him off at the pass. The money I'd raised outside the office had matched the money raised inside the office since I'd first closed Fritz all those months back. And to be honest I didn't want to be office bound once again just because Al had decided he was going to run the restaurant, I was having way too much fun outside the office. And after all, hooker leads didn't develop themselves. I'd often meet with Lana and Daria, usually in restaurants. These meetings were time consuming yet enjoyable, but more importantly productive. I think Al just thought that hooker leads just happened, or that if they took any developing at all it wouldn't take much time and could be done outside of daylight hours. He never declared this openly but I sensed that's how he felt. We agreed that between us we'd cover everything, besides L.E.S was an evening only joint, so I figured Al could still base operations from behind his desk in the office during the day, and maybe even leave the flower buying to Penka.

Our absence from the office for long periods while we were overseeing the renovation and busily involved in all that garbage took its toll. We couldn't have it both ways it seemed. The discord due to our absence over that period had not come to a head until now. It'd been like a poison festering away. While the cat's away the mice will play, and five of them packed their cheese and buggered off. So much for pirate loyalty. I wasn't that surprised if the truth be known, I was well aware our leadership was crucial and I'd ignored that fact. I'd taken for granted their loyalty and assumed that these guys would totally self-manage. Or at least I'd kidded myself of this. Fifty percent of our crew, gone. The blame fell squarely at mine and Al's door. We'd taken our eye off the ball and we paid the price. So we were down to five closers in an office set-up for ten. Recruiting new people was a real hassle and there were also rumours around that various authorities were infiltrating rooms and ultimately busting them. Bringing known journeymen in was also a pain in the butt, they saw themselves as superstars and acted up, when the truth was they were mostly washed out and useless, hardly picking up the phone and distracting the rest of the room with their bullshit war stories. It was time to make plans.

I took the guys to an Irish bar the following morning for breakfast to either establish their loyalty, as best as I could in this skullduggery business, or to find out if it was time to call it a day. All five swore their allegiance and actually seemed happy the other five had jumped ship. A growing divide between the two groups had apparently been bubbling away beneath the surface, but not noticed by Al or I as our attention had been elsewhere. Not good, and ultimately had caused a mutiny. Satisfied that I had five guys that wanted to move forward it was back to the office and all hands on deck. As I've previously explained, I'd rather burn an empty desk than have it staring at me all day like a lost puppy. Burning though, wasn't really an option, so my remaining crew dismantled them an left them alongside one of the recycling skips close by. Within an hour the desks had disappeared. The remaining desks, spaced out accordingly, looked fine. The guys seemed jacked-up about the even more streamlined operation and the money machine fired back up.

Al meantime was reprimanding cleaning staff at L.E.S for not having polished the underside of the bar stools sufficiently, or something equally as trivial and bizarre under the circumstances.

I'd quickly come to realise that L.E.S was never going to give us the type of returns we'd be satisfied with, far from it, and I knew instinctively it was already time stamped. Our running costs were high and often takings didn't meet our 'no expense spared' outgoings, meaning the office was subsidising what I had now come to think of as Al's sinking ship. I understood of course that a new business took time to develop but even so, we were jam packed Thursday, Friday and Saturday so I didn't really see where the potential for growth and added revenue lay. So what actually had we managed to do? Well, in a nutshell we'd pumped a million into toy and in the process lost half our pirates. Nice.

I wasn't going down with this sinking ship, but fuck, if I'd rammed all this dough into this fancy cake I sure as hell was going to take a big bite out of it where the fun stakes were concerned. And although Al had taken on the responsibility of overseeing operations we'd generally spend our Monday, Tuesday and Wednesday evenings in the downstairs cocktail bar, that was closed to the public early week, slugging back liquor. It was a cool little haven that would fit about a hundred at a squeeze and had a fantastic club atmosphere on the busy nights of the week due in no small part to the excellent up and coming DJ's we'd hire that got the party rocking in our subterranean den of iniquity. But like I said, early week this became mine and Al's private bar. We had a huge mirror on the wall that at the click of a remote turned into a TV that never failed to impress any guests we invited to join us in our private den to watch a game, eat, drink and generally get merry. I had many memorable nights at L.E.S and just as with the hooker lead stories I could fill a whole book glamourising those immoral happenings as well. I once met the girlfriend of a German racing driver through some of our cool gay regulars, she insisted I escort her to the bathroom where she further insisted she snort a line of coke from my old boy. Strangely, when I invited her back to my place she refused saying she never cheated on her boyfriend. Germans!

I had a friend visit from the UK who'd worked with me in various locations on the dark side before seeing the light and returning to the real world. He'd brought his new girlfriend with him and delighted in embarrassing her by letting me know he'd met her on a certain dating site. Privately, he'd told me he'd had an absolute whale of a time with numerous girls before he came across his 'keeper'. My inquisitive nature led me to checking out this site, and it wasn't long before I was messaging back and forth with a girl from Vladivostok. She obviously wasn't currently located in that far eastern outpost, but rattling around Barcelona instead. Our messaging led to a phone conversation, which in turn led to a date. Not giving anything away I asked if she knew L.E.S and suggested that we should meet there.

The tall blonde looked like a sexy, yet serious KGB agent, and showed up right on time. Looking back now it's as if I was living somebody else's life. I wasn't disappointed in the slightest with Sasha, she was even more attractive in the flesh than her very well presented photos on the dating site had suggested. The dinner went well and as I'd planned she was suitably impressed when I broke the news that this was in fact my restaurant. Outside, was not the easiest place to park but this night the gods had been smiling on me and I'd managed to find a spot directly out front. When I opened the passenger door for this very fit looking leggy blond to climb in, I knew it was all over bar the shouting. A hole in one was anticipated and scored forthwith.

I saw Sasha several times after that night, she did however start taking about marriage within four or five weeks which kind of put a damper on things. I'd been up front in all my friendships with the opposite sex where my long term intentions were concerned, or lack of them rather. That's probably why it was such an easy relationship with Lana. We didn't expect anything from each other on that front. Regardless of what anyone thinks about my playboy lifestyle I never cheated on my girlfriend – I didn't have one. Al on the other hand cheated on Penka at every opportunity, which I could never fully get my head around. He was much older than her, and she was a great looking and loyal girl I'd always thought. One of my strangest and possibly most memorable experiences in L.E.S however involved the not so loyal, but delicious Penka.

Mine and Al's business relationship and friendship was being put under a great deal of pressure and was starting to crumble, as I continued to bring in the money and Al played out his fantasy as the suave and sophisticated restaurateur, lapping it up on centre stage at L.E.S. Every time I suggested that our businesses would benefit all round if he did what he did best and let Penka run the show at L.E.S he'd make excuse after excuse as to why L.E.S needed him, when the actual reality is that L.E.S needed him like it needed a fire, or a flood.

Additional unrest was created when, after returning from a trip to the Philippines I discovered that someone had let themselves into my apartment and helped themselves to twenty thousand euros I had stashed for emergencies. The only person that knew about this cash was Al, as he'd taken the same precaution of keeping emergency cash in his gaff should he have to bolt. To this day I cannot prove anything and Al at the time had his reasons as to why he thought one of the closers who'd left in the exodus had been the guilty party. My apartment was not broken into however and the only other person with a key had been my old buddy. But as unreasonable as it seemed to me, my gut told me that good old Al had sticky fingered my twenty big 'uns. I was pissed off but did what I always did, I picked up the phone and replaced the money in my life that had been fluttered away, or in this case, lifted. And these days I was purely hitting my hooker leads.

Al in the meantime was hitting up the girls we had working at L.E.S. This was not the smartest of moves when his live in girlfriend co-managed the place. I think they call it shitting on your own doorstep. It was an early Wednesday evening and I'd invited the crew for an impromptu knees up at L.E.S. Lana was on vacation somewhere, Mallorca I think, with a Swedish client so I'd asked the Ukrainian along with some of her friends to join the party. Daria was a social butterfly and as mid-week was generally the quite time for these girls, jumped on the invitation.

We kept the party upstairs as the restaurant had a full glass frontage and it was always good for business if passersby could see the fun being had inside and decide to join in. And there was plenty going on. There were phone pirates, hookers, a few straight regulars, a few gay regulars, non-hookers looking as if they were up for some action, beautiful staff were joining in, there were cocktails galore and pretty much no one had an appetite having quashed the desire for food through the snorting of the devil's dandruff. The music was chilled but heavily bass influenced which always supports a great buzz. Al was holding court telling one of his outrageous tales, a whopper about him having joined the circus as a boy or something as equally unlikely. Laughter erupted at whatever punchline he'd delivered, and it was all good. Al motioned to me as he peeled away from the group. It transpired he wanted me to distract Penka as he had a dead cert lined up with one of the girls and he planned on taking her into a rear store room for a little slap and tickle. “A bit close to home isn’t it Al?” I said, not really wanting to act as a decoy in this ridiculous plan, though I wasn’t going to get on my high horse either, he was perfectly capable of making his own decisions and fucking up of his own accord. His plan involved him and I retiring to the downstairs bar to privately smoke a bone, taking a break from the madness that was being enjoyed by all upstairs. He’d ask Penka to come down to serve us drinks and to share the joint with us. He’d arranged for one of the closers to call his cell phone ten minutes into our departure below. His plan on receiving the call was to excuse himself, zip back up the stairs and to disappear into the store room with his ‘dead cert’. It wasn’t really my idea of fun baby-sitting his girl while he was galavanting around like a Viking, but I agreed all the same, as he seemed so excited at the prospect, and perhaps the turn on for him was the danger to which he was exposing himself and knowing he'd manipulated and manufactured a situation which involved him controlling several players in his theatre of deceit. The three of us sat in a triangular formation at barstools in front of our Italian marble topped downstairs bar, Penka having joined us after serving our drinks. Al was dressed in black suede loafers, black jeans and a black shirt open at the collar. All this black was set off by a gold Rolex watch. He looked like the Duke of darkness. Penka matched him perfectly in a black Prada cotton dress cut just above the knee and black heels. Her female version of Al's gold Rolex setting off her classic look beautifully. Penka was a fine looking woman who always carried a tan, she had long smooth legs, a high full bottom, ample breasts and a slim waist. Why Al was chasing the help was beyond me. I'm sure Al would be considered a good catch by some, but Penka would as well, and certainly by a lot more.

As planned his cell phone chirped to life with the theme tune from the Godfather. He did a fairly good job of pretending to be having a real conversation, and made it sound like the group upstairs wanted an encore from Al the great story teller, and were chomping at the bit for another of his outlandish tales. He did tell a pretty funny story, I must admit. But all this of course was academic as he had no intention of blasting into rhetoric amongst his waiting fans, his blasting intentions lay in the broom cupboard at the back of the gaff.

"He must think I'm an idiot" Penka said as he flew up the stairs two at a time. "Sorry?" I was trying my hardest to look like I hadn't a clue what she was on about, but knowing full well it was useless trying to pull the wool over the sultry Bulgarian's eyes. “Oh come on, don’t you treat me like an idiot too”. She didn’t seem upset or angry, she just didn’t want to appear like an unknowing idiot, which was fair enough. I shrugged and gave her a half smile, almost apologetically as if to say, what can I tell you? She read my expression perfectly and told me not to worry and offered her glass up to touch mine. We sat silently, though not awkwardly, it was as if we’d reached some mutual understanding. We had formed an unwitting alliance. The dynamic had shifted somewhat. We continued to sip our drinks in the dimly lit bar, occasionally making eye contact. Then on one occasion she caught it as my eyes dropped to her extremely attractive cleavage for a split second. Immediately she raised a shapely eyebrow, giving me the ‘oh yeah mister’ look. I just gave another shrug and half smile before taking another sip of my drink. What she did next took me completely by surprise. Maintaining eye contact she reached over and gently picked up my wrist before dropping it lightly on her right thigh, parted her knees slightly and leaned back on her bar stool, dropped her gaze to my hand questioningly, before returning her gaze to my eyes expectantly. No, surely this wasn't happening, I thought, but quite obviously it was. I thought fleetingly about the twenty grand that had gone missing from my apartment, I thought about what a dick Al had been in sacking Frankie and deciding to run the place himself, I thought about how he'd put me in this situation right now, and ultimately I thought fuck it, as I slid my hand up Penka's inner thigh. This situation was so unexpected yet had become so sexually charged that it seemed to be out of my control.

I touched Al's girlfriend for probably no more than three minutes until she achieved her climax and moved my hand away, but the thing had been such a massive turn on. She straightened herself out and climbed off the bar stool on unstable legs, disappeared around the other side of the bar and prepared me another drink. Returning with it she acted as if nothing had happened and was as cool as a cucumber. We touched glasses again just as I heard Al's footsteps bounding down the metal dogleg staircase we'd had installed that was meant to represent the fire escape stairways so prevalent on the outside of buildings on the lower east side in New York. "Those guys" Al joked as he bounded over to join us, "wanna do a bump?" He said as he sat down, "sure, why not" I said, as he brought out a small baggie. Penka excused herself to return to operations on top deck leaving me to listen to Al's failed attempt with the 'bitch' he'd felt sure was up for it, but had ended up being nothing more than a prick teaser .Talk about a plan backfiring!

I knew now for sure that mine and Al's business relationship and friendship was about to come to a sticky end.

The writing was clearly on the wall as far as I was concerned. There had been too much suspicion, too much deceit , and like Penka, I wasn't stupid or blind either. All things, good or bad, come to and end, and I could without doubt feel change was in the air. To be honest, I didn't even care. Like any pirate worth his eye patch and parrot, I'd ride out this coming storm like I'd always done, and as the saying goes, as one door closes another one opens.

As L.E.S entered its second year of trading the novelty had completely worn off, for me. I was sick to the back teeth of the sight of the place. There was a tension between Al and I during daylight hours that always seemed to dissolve when the sun went down and we put our drinking hats on, only to re-emerge the following morning. Al's determination to soldier on with L.E.S was admirable, but there comes a time when stubborn determination is not enough, and I'm a great believer in the saying that if you keep doing what you always did you'll keep getting what you always got. And I couldn't see what we were doing differently to change L.E.S's financial fortunes. The long and the short of it was that I wanted out. I was tired of raising money from the other thing to finance some idiotic fantasy Al held of being this successful restaurant owner, when all I saw was a centre of attention seeking wannabe superstar. The whole enterprise had been a mistake.

I went to work behind the scenes, I needed to formulate a plan, and I needed to do it now. I was happy that there'd been no awkward situations with Penka since Fingergate, she behaved like absolutely nothing had happened which was a relief and made easier by the fact that I didn't see Penka unless she was by Al's side, either fleetingly in the office or at the restaurant. I was spending far less time at L.E.S too, and more time socialising with my guys, treating them to dinner regularly at Gauchos Argentinian Steak House, the old favourite, on Calle Aragon. A pirate's favourite for sure. Sushi is fine, especially when dining with a beautiful woman, but pirate bonding is best achieved tearing into bloody red meat. My pal Jeff had also come along to some of these dinners, a hugely likeable character who always inspired others for better or worse depending on your perspective. My guys took to him instantly. We were all Brits and all cut from the same cloth. I knew exactly what I was doing. Likewise, Jeff took to my guys and confessed to me that he'd get rid of his partner, Tricky Trev, who Jeff felt brought nothing to the table, in a heartbeat if I gave him the word. "Hold that thought Jeff" I told him, "stranger things have happened". I was nurturing my guys loyalty and preparing for the change I could now smell in the air. I didn't need to bad mouth Al in the slightest, not my style, but the guys intimated privately without any coercion on my part that they felt badly let down by him. I knew what they meant. They also felt Penka was a jumped up bitch who'd exerted her influence over Al unfavourably where the pirates were concerned. It would have been incredible to watch their faces if I'd recounted the finger fuck story, but that, I didn't do. Information is power, if that kind of information got out into the gossipsphere it could only spell trouble. I also made sure Al knew I was taking good care of our guys, the last thing I needed was him finding out I was wining and dining these guys behind his back and manufacturing a situation where I would divide and conquer. Then Al did it again. Set himself up unwittingly that is. He confided in me that the girl he'd intended getting into the storeroom was still up for it, and the reason she'd not ventured into the mop store with Al is that she'd not wanted to appear cheap, or an easy lay. She lived up the coast in a small town on the Costa Brava, about 30 minutes from Girona, an hour of so drive from Barcelona. Al's latest plan was to jump in his Range Rover and hightail it up north on the understanding he was meeting some friends who were flying out of Girona airport the following morning. He'd spend the night within them, then take them to the airport the next day. Or so Penka was meant to believe. What a hero. He asked me to hang out at the restaurant to keep an eye on things, which I thought was a really, really bad idea, but didn't voice that opinion. This could only end in tears.

It was fairly busy for a Sunday night and I was pleased to see Penka, looking her usual glamorous self, busily taking care of business and schmoozing with the regulars. When we did speak she didn't press me about Al's trip up the coast and I assumed she knew what he was up to and perhaps didn't even care. Either way she didn't seem to me like she was carrying the weight of the world on her shoulders and I witnessed plenty of laughing, smiling and flirting with the Sunday evening crowd.

It started raining which always had the effect of driving a few passersby in through the doors and keeping existing patrons inside. The combined effect favourable, and before too long the feeling wasn't too dissimilar to a Saturday night. I vacated my seat at the bar to make way for a group recently arrived from the sudden downpour. There was no one I felt like engaging in conversation so I slinked away from the bar and decided to head to the privacy of the downstairs bar and smoke a bone, perhaps there'd be a game on the mirror TV.

I was no sooner behind the bar pouring myself a rum and coke on the rocks when I heard the distinctive footfall of female steps coming down the metal stairs. No prizes for guessing who. Flashes of our previous sexual encounter flooded my mind as she approached wearing a very mischievous smile. She closed in on me without any hesitation and gently put her hand on my chest, pushing me back against the far wall. "I owe you" is all she said before dropping to her knees. And moments later all I could think was 'holy cow, this girl has absolutely no gag reflex'. And not long after that we were sat at the bar having a post sexual encounter drink.

Later that night she insisted she accompany me home where I rode her like I was racing in the Kentucky Derby. Sorry about that Al. The following morning I decided that was it. I wanted out. A few days later sat in the downstairs bar with my business partner that I had now suddenly realised I despised, listening to his recounting of his conquest up north like he was some sort of an invading marauder, I lay my cards on the table. I wasn't going to keep subsidising L.E.S and I wasn't prepared to keep paying him fifty percent of our ill-gotten gains when he was basically a sad, failing restaurant manager these days. I suggested was we put L.E.S on the market and cut our losses and get back to what we did best. I didn't for one minute envision us getting back to what we knew best together, but didn't feel the need to drop this in the mix at this stage. Al's initial response was to attack and to threaten, which he knew perfectly well was a pointless exercise. He'd seen me under attack many times over the years and knew I didn't buckle easily. In fact I didn't buckle period. He reminded me that he, and he alone, had the connection for the stocks and a few other important cogs to the machine, but must have been delusional if he thought I hadn't solutions to any of these things. I had everything I needed waiting in the wings. Why take a chance? I'd already cut him off at the pass.

The long and short of our discussions were that he wanted to keep L.E.S and was basically prepared to walk away from the office. All well and good but we'd collectively injected seven figures into this project. I got valuations for L.E.S as a going concern and for selling the traspaso (business lease) and the figure wasn't anywhere near the amount we'd pumped into this dump, as I now felt about this albatross around my neck. Two hundred and fifty, if we were lucky.

Al paid me fifty grand and I walked away, able to get back to what I knew, with the burden off myshoulders and free of that bad relationship that had started to stink like shit. All the goings-on, all the suspicion, all the deceit and all the bad feelings generated between the pair of us had now come to a head.

And if only Al had been true to his word when we wished each other well and shook on our deal things would have been fine. But that's not what happened. I'd taken the hit on the restaurant and walked away in good faith, so when it got back to me that good old Al was attempting to rally the troops against me it didn't fill me with happy smiley thoughts. L.E.S was a sinking ship. It wasn't making any money and he couldn't sell it without my agreement. Now I'd never agree to selling that piece of shit. That ship had sailed. The gloves were off.

Afterword – A Message from the Author.

Although this story is a work of fiction it is based around a network of events that actually occurred. People may assume I am the lead character in this novel as it is written from a first person perspective. I am not. I have no idea if there are any such thing as hooker leads, and I've never had any kind of sexual encounter with any of my business partner's girlfriends. I didn't bump into a high class call girl outside the Rolex shop and I've never owned a Porsche. I'm highlighting just a few of these fictional ideas to demonstrate that this work is one of fiction and not a biography.

Nonetheless, I was involved in the operation of a boiler room as the media have referred to it. Arrested, extradited, charged and subsequently was sentenced to six years in a federal prison for my role in this illegal operation. I'm by no means glamourising the behaviour of the characters in this novel and do not condone the immoral behaviour of those characters.

The underlying message in this book is intended to be one of caution. There are still plenty of operations out there conducting their unscrupulous operations. I know this as a fact as I have been approached since leaving prison by a few asking if I need 'work', and offering to fly me out to such far flung places as Cyprus, Thailand and Indonesia, where they hope to avoid detection and prosecution. People are still sending their hard earned savings to these crooks and if this book serves as a warning to one person and stops them from losing their life savings I'll consider it a success.

Visit my website and subscribe for updates, new releases and stories about my prison journey: http://phonepirate.net

11631228R00143

Printed in Great Britain
by Amazon